NOT SO HAPPILY EVER AFTER

Reader praise for "Not So Happily Ever After":

"Easily the best book written on King Ludwig II in this decade."

"I finished your book on King Ludwig II last night. It was so moving. Even though I was familiar with the story and knew the ending, a tear was still brought to my eye when he was found. I learned things I didn't know and your epilogue was perfect ... I believe anyone reading it would be able to see Germany and the castles through their mind's eye just by your descriptive word."

"This book is a must read! I have always been fascinated with the 'Mad King' but didn't know a lot about him, but now I can claim myself among the many that have at least some little knowledge of him and his fantastic life. The author was very good in explaining the complex and introverted life of this most intelligent and exacting man!"

"I very much enjoyed reading this book. I thought that the author was quirky and fun and I enjoyed the history lesson wrapped into a fairy tale. Her description of Kind Ludwig's castles was point on. Reading her description of Neuschwanstein made me feel as though I was there again. This is an enjoyable book and a must read for anyone that will be traveling to Bavaria and making a visit to any of King Ludwig's castles."

"In preparing visit to Germany I went looking for a book on King Ludwig, the Bavarian King. This fine book completed his life with extremely interesting facts. I am now prepared to visit his castles with many stories that bring King Ludwig to reality. Thank you, this book is a winner!"

"I was visiting castles in Bavaria and this book helped bring the history of the castles and palaces I visited. I would definitely recommend."

"Wish I had read this before or during my trip to Bavaria and Ludwig's Castles. It still was exciting reading for me because it brings history to life. Fascinating, informative."

Not So Happily Ever After

The Tale of King Ludwig II

Susan Barnett Braun

CreateSpace

Published by CreateSpace

ISBN: 978-1-4774-9453-0

Typesetting services by BOOKOW.COM

CONTENTS

Bavaria

Würzburg

Bayreuth

Nuremberg

Regensburg

R. Danube

R. Isar

N

Augsburg

Landshut

R. Lech

R. Inn

Munich

Starnberg
Berg Castle

Chiemsee

Neuschwanstein
Castle

Herrenchiemsee Palace

Füssen

Linderhof
Castle

Hohenschwangau
Castle

0   50   100 km

PROLOGUE

Once upon a time, there was a handsome prince. He loved to build, so when he grew up to be king, he built his own castle. The castle was fabulous, with spires and towers and winding staircases, and even an artificial cave inside. His creation was called Neuschwanstein (Noy-SCHVAHN-shtine), and it was so wonderful that it inspired even the master of imagination, Walt Disney. The Cinderella Castle at Disney World and the Sleeping Beauty Castle at Disneyland are each based on the king's fairy tale creation.

Sadly, the king who designed Neuschwanstein is no longer here to walk through its gateway. He didn't even live to see his fairy tale castle completed, because …

Well, I'm getting ahead of myself. Let's just say that he lived not so happily ever after. This is his tale.

CHAPTER 1

Ludwig Otto Friedrich Wilhelm

ONCE UPON A TIME ...

The people of Bavaria were overjoyed. 101 cannon shots and innumerable pealing church bells pierced the summer Munich skies. It was August 25, 1845, and a baby had been born to Crown Princess Marie and her husband, Maximilian II. Someday Maximilian would become king, and someday after that, this new baby would lead the kingdom of Bavaria. Since baby girls were not considered good candidates for kingship, the birth of a boy was always a joyful relief. This new baby was named Otto.

But wait! This is a book about King Ludwig, not King Otto. That's right. But the fact is, King Ludwig II spent the first few days of his life named Otto. Why the name change?

Maximilian's father, Bavarian King Ludwig I, came to visit his grandson. He informed the new parents that the baby had been born on his own fifty-ninth birthday. Additionally, August 25 was the feast day of Saint Ludwig, the patron saint of Bavaria. How could the baby not be named Ludwig? So the name was changed, and little Ludwig (LOOT-vikh, by the way) began life named after the current king, his grandfather.

Although he didn't know it, baby Ludwig had several strikes against him already. Both his mother and his father came from families with much intermarriage. For instance, his mother's parents were cousins and her grandmothers were sisters. It was common at the time for royalty and other aristocratic families to intermarry, as a way to keep all their power and money within the family. But intermarriage has serious downsides. Children born to people related to each other are more likely to inherit a variety of problems, since recessive traits may exist in both parents already.

And the Wittelsbachs (this was the name of the Bavarian royal family) certainly had their share of recessive traits. On the positive side, Wittelsbachs tended to be artistic and intelligent. Ludwig's grandfather, Ludwig I, loved architecture. Much of modern Munich owes its classical architectural beauty to him. He designed the grand street known as Ludwigstraße and the giant three-arched victory gate, called Siegestor.

Ludwig's father, Maximilian II, was more retiring and shy than his own father had been. He loved intellectual discussions and once remarked that he would have enjoyed being a university professor had he not been born into royalty.

Unfortunately, the negative aspects of the Wittelsbachs tended to outweigh the positives. Wittelsbachs tended to be stubbornly determined, and they lacked the flexibility that is necessary to rule wisely. The entire family was generously described as "eccentric," and certain relatives were famous for their odd traits: Ludwig's aunt Alexandra spent much of her life convinced that she had swallowed a glass piano. She insisted that the piano remained inside her, causing her understandable distress. Her sister, Ludwig's aunt Marie, was obsessed with cleanliness. She would only wear white clothes so that she could easily spot any bit of dirt.

Ludwig's family tree was full of interlocking branches. Numerous relatives were considered insane, which was the label given to many different mental illnesses during that time. One relative had even married her own nephew! With such a heritage, what did the future hold for Ludwig? No doubt his parents were curious.

CHAPTER 2

Ludwig and his family, around 1860

... THERE LIVED AN IMAGINATIVE PRINCE

Almost three years after Ludwig's birth, his parents were given another chance to use the name Otto when a second baby boy was born. Otto Wilhelm Luitpold Adalbert Waldemar arrived April 27, 1848.

While Otto's arrival was a joyous occasion, it was overshadowed by current events. His grandfather, Ludwig I, had given up the throne just a month earlier. Why? He had become fascinated with an Irish dancer named Lola Montez. Ludwig I showered her with so much money and attention that his fellow citizens decided they'd be better off with another king. The saying "whatever Lola wants, Lola gets" originates from this situation.

Ludwig I was forced to abdicate, and his son Maximilian became king. Ludwig was now crown prince of Bavaria – second in line to the throne, at less than three years old.

Bavaria was not a country, but a state in the southern part of what we now call Germany. It covered an area about the size of West Virginia, and had a population of four million at the time.

Toddler Ludwig was unaware of all this. He spent his earliest days happily roaming the family home, Hohenschwangau Castle (Ho-un-SHVAHN-gow). The castle sat nestled in the Bavarian mountains, seventy miles from the bustling capital, Munich. Ludwig's father, Max, had fallen in love with the ruins of the castle years before. Perhaps the faint echo of his ancestors, who had lived there earlier, drew him to the site. He gazed out at the two serene lakes nearby and decided that Hohenschwangau (meaning "high country of the swan") would be the idea country retreat for his family.

Max restored the restful yellow walls of the castle, topping them with red tiled roofs and medieval-looking crenellations. Fountains splashed in outdoor courtyards decked with roses.

But Ludwig was most affected by the castle's interior. Here Max hired Bavarian artists to paint huge, life-like murals across every wall, hallway, and even much of the furniture. Tales of German history and folktales of heroic legendary characters came to life in these colorful scenes. Little Ludwig "read" the history of his Wittelsbach ancestors as he gazed by the hour at these hypnotic illustrations. Knights, swans, and water seemed to surround him everywhere he looked, and these things brought him comfort and inspiration his entire life. From Lohengrin the legendary swan knight to the crusader Tannhäuser, whom legend placed in the original Hohenschwangau castle, Ludwig was surrounded by dreamy legends and myths. It became his misfortune that he preferred these to real life.

Young Ludwig was the definition of an introvert, drawing energy from being alone and feeling drained when he was forced to be around others. Carl

Jung, famous psychologist of the early twentieth century, said, "There is no such thing as a pure introvert. Such a man would be in the lunatic asylum." However, Ludwig came as close to pure introversion as was humanly possible. He disliked the company of other children, owing both to his natural temperament and also to his parents' desire to bring him up isolated and set-apart, since he would one day become king. He stared repeatedly at the Germans legends depicted on his home walls, and once a guest observed him sitting alone in silence.

"Your Highness should have something read to you, which would help pass these boring hours," he said.

"But I am not bored at all!" Ludwig replied. "I imagine various things and keep myself quite amused."

Ludwig enjoyed dressing up in costumes. His mother, who was Catholic, noticed Ludwig dressing as a nun on several occasions. His black robes brushing the ground, the young prince visited the private chapels in his family's palaces. There he sat for hours, fascinated with the paintings and dramatic gold décor of the altars and the vaulted ceilings.

As with many other childhood hobbies, Ludwig's love of costumes continued into his adulthood. In many ways, he remained a child even as an adult. He liked creating plays with a puppet theater, where he would recreate dramatic scenes from German history. Although Ludwig and his mother were never very close, he did love hearing her tell myths and folktales to him. Marie wrote that Ludwig "listened with delight when I told him Bible stories and showed him pictures from them, especially the story of the good Samaritan." Other favorite stories featured swans, and swans became one of Ludwig's lifelong favorites.

One hobby Ludwig did not enjoy was playing soldiers. This bothered his parents, as they felt that a future king should show an interest in military matters. Younger brother Otto loved battle play, and this, along with his warm, friendly personality, made him the favorite of both parents. Otto loved being around people as much as Ludwig disliked it. Otto also loved hunting, a hobby the sensitive Ludwig detested. The boys' teachers whispered among themselves that it was a pity that Otto would not be king someday rather than Ludwig. Otto's personality and interests seemed much more suitable for kingship than did Ludwig's.

In an attempt to mold Ludwig into a more suitable future king, Maximilian treated his older son more harshly than Otto, who was indulged. Ludwig observed this difference, but instead of becoming tougher, he grew discouraged and began to dislike his father. "Otto is a good boy, and I will be good also," he once wrote, pitifully, to his mother. But neither Ludwig nor his father's opinion changed much. Throughout his life, Ludwig's attempts to change and "be good" in others' eyes were largely unsuccessful. Maybe this is why he eventually gave up trying, and retreated into his own imaginary world.

Ludwig's favorite childhood interest involved building. He was thrilled to receive blocks as a gift from his grandfather, and spent hours creating various structures with them. At seven, he built a copy of the Siegestor victory gate his grandfather had designed. He also built a replica of the Holy Sepulchre, where Jesus was thought to have been buried. He illuminated this with a flame, which he tended conscientiously.

Ludwig excitedly wrote to his mother about another building project, this one involving his science teacher: "Near our little brook the Count and I built a little group of rocks and we conducted the hose, which Liebig gave me, through it. If we pour some water into the hose it runs out of the rocks and looks like a well, and this stands for the water which Moses struck out of the rock with the rod of Horeb. The Count cut the tablets of stone in wood and I wrote the Commandments on them."

Childhood also introduced Ludwig to another lifelong passion: horses and horseback riding. Horses were more than animals to Ludwig: they were friends. Both in childhood and throughout later life, he enjoyed riding horses through the Bavarian mountains. Ludwig was an excellent horse-man, even as a boy.

Always missing from Ludwig's life was the love of his parents. Marie had married her thirty-four-year-old groom just three days shy of her seventeenth birthday, and she had Ludwig when she was just nineteen. She had little life experience and seems to have tried her best with her children. However, that "best" often meant spending just an hour a day with them when they were very young. Meals were the only time each day when the boys regularly saw their parents. Both Max and Marie had been raised this way themselves, and did not see it as unusual.

King Max's cabinet secretary remarked, "The Queen had little knowledge as to how to draw her little sons to her. She visited them only fleetingly in their rooms, and scarcely even knew how to treat them as children ought to be treated. Nor did the little sons know how to treat their mother."

Queen Marie was not intellectually curious and once proudly declared, "I never open a book, and I don't understand how anyone can incessantly read." This placed her interests directly opposite those of Ludwig, and as the years went by the two had little in common.

Unfortunately, Ludwig's father was not any warmer toward his boys. In keeping with the Victorian standards of the day, he wanted them raised in a cold, strict manner in hopes of building strength and character. This approach failed with both boys. One of Max's officials wrote, "He [Max] rarely visited the rooms where [Ludwig and Otto] were growing up; when he did he usually just held out his hand in greeting and took his leave as quickly as possible. It needed long and hard efforts to persuade the King to take his eldest son with him on his morning walk in the English Garden." Max disapproved of Ludwig's sensitive, romantic nature, and tried to distance himself from his son. As a result, their relationship was always strained.

A typical day in Ludwig's childhood involved waking at 5:30 and spending an hour on homework before breakfast. The boys took cold baths, which were thought to calm "over-excitement," and were given little food to eat. Ludwig's elderly childhood nurse reported frequently sneaking bits of food to the nursery for the hungry boys.

Ludwig's first teacher was a young woman named Sybille Meilhaus. Caring and nurturing, she treated Ludwig with more warmth and affection than he received from anyone else. He remained close to her until she died in 1881, writing her letters and confiding in her more than he ever did his own mother.

Although Fräulein Meilhaus tried to instill good character traits in Ludwig, at times she was frustrated by his attitudes. On a shopping trip, Meilhaus once spied Ludwig stealing a small purse in two of his favorite colors, blue and silver. When she confronted him about this outside the store, Ludwig was stubborn and not a bit apologetic: "What have I done wrong? Why should it be a sin? One day I will be king of this country, and all that belongs to my subjects belongs to me."

Otto often suffered from Ludwig's sense of royal entitlement. Once, Ludwig tied his younger brother up, and, in a prelude to similar threats he would make to future servants, announced plans to behead him. Thankfully, an aide intervened.

On another occasion, a servant found Otto coughing from strangulation by a rope that Ludwig had twisted around his neck! Asked why he had done such a thing, Ludwig was indignant. "This is no business of yours! This is my vassal and he has dared to resist my will! He must be executed!" The servant rescued Otto, and Max gave Ludwig a sound beating. Punishments such as these were etched deeply in Ludwig's mind for the rest of his life. He had very little sense of humor and took life seriously. No joking around for Ludwig!

When Fräulein Meilhaus left the royal household to get married, a former military officer named Count de la Rosee became nine-year-old Ludwig's teacher. His strict, old-fashioned teachings did little to temper Ludwig's insistence that only his opinion mattered.

De la Rosee worked with Ludwig's father to plan a rigorous schedule of education for Ludwig, with the goal being that the crown prince would learn "to think." When Ludwig was eleven, his education intensified. The schooling that normal German students completed in eight years was planned for Ludwig to finish in just five (although this was eventually extended to seven years). Ludwig studied six days each week, only taking a break on Sundays.

Michael Klass, brought in to instruct Ludwig in grammar and German, reinforced the idea that Ludwig was special. He taught the prince that there was a link between royalty and God, and helped Ludwig cement the thinking that he was "God's anointed" and superior to other people by nature of his birth.

Add this to de la Rosee's insistence that Ludwig be addressed as Royal Highness and that all household servants should bow to him, even though the royal family declared these things unnecessary until the prince reached age eighteen. With all this adoration, it's easy to see how Ludwig's ego became quite inflated.

Ludwig's sense of importance is understandable considering how isolated he was during his formative years. De la Rosee taught that he should trust no one, since nobody could understand his role as crown prince. He also insisted that Ludwig and Otto could only associate with other members of royalty, so he effectively cut off the boys from making any friends in the outside world. Add this to Max's directive that the boys could not play with girls, and imagine how isolated they were from reality and from their future subjects. This fueled an already quiet and melancholy personality such as Ludwig's. Yet de la Rosee insisted that Ludwig should "be kept from brooding; he must not linger over disagreeable impressions but try to be less sensitive towards them."

This was almost impossible for Ludwig, who was shy and sensitive by nature as well. He spent his days lingering over his many thoughts, or picking out tunes on his piano. Some nights, he loved to ride his horse mile after mile throughout the remote countryside, deep in thought. Other nights found him rowing a boat across one of the lakes near Hohenschwangau, reciting poetry aloud. Given his solitary upbringing, it's to Ludwig's credit that his mother noted "from childhood he liked giving presents to others from his own money and possessions." His generosity stayed with him throughout his life.

Ludwig's excellent memory and thoughtful nature led him to love reading and history, since they fueled his imagination. He became fluent in French, studied Latin, and learned enough English to read Shakespeare's *Romeo and Juliet.* He was not as fond of math and science, with their exact nature. His teachers also encouraged physical fitness, and this came easily to the prince with his love of nature, hiking, boating, and horseback riding. De la Rosee encouraged him to develop a strong will and to be obedient, although Ludwig's ideas about the superiority of his position prevented him from ever obeying, except out of fear. Ludwig did fear both his father and his teacher, and he obeyed them based on this alone.

Teachers and other household members noted the eccentric behavior of both princes. The royal physician observed that even as a young child, Otto was prone to serious hallucinations in which he was convinced he saw and heard things that were not really there. Ludwig had similar, though less serious, tendencies. The doctor noted an occasion where the prince was playing billiards and claimed he heard voices taunting him. Rumors began to circulate through the royal court that the boys had inherited the famous Wittelsbach "eccentricity."

The princes' isolation led to several difficulties, one being that they had no sense of the value of money. Ludwig was given a monthly allowance, and often spent it in a single day without even realizing it. Otto, being the younger son, received less. He heard once that dentists would pay for healthy teeth, and he offered the court dentist several of his own teeth in an attempt to earn spending money. When Max learned of this, he had Otto beaten.

When Ludwig turned eighteen, he suddenly went from having very little money to having access to millions. He had no idea of how to budget this money well, and this led to the troubles that plagued the last part of his life. Could things have ended better for Ludwig had he learned to spend money wisely? Could he have related to his people better had he been allowed to associate with them when he was a child? Could his life have felt less tortured had his parents and teachers recognized his sensitive spirit and treated him gently rather than harshly? Could he have been a more effective leader if he considered himself the equal of his subjects, instead of feeling superior to them?

We will never know.

CHAPTER 3

Ludwig as Lohengrin, the Swan Knight

FAIRY TALES COME TO LIFE

Sometimes, a single event can change the course of a life. This was true for Ludwig. On February 2, 1861, he attended a performance of the opera *Lohengrin.*

If you're thinking, *an opera performance wouldn't change* my *life*, I won't disagree. But you're not Ludwig, and these are different times.

As Ludwig reached his teenage years, his personality and appearance remained remarkably similar to the way they had been in his childhood. He was still stubborn, vain, and handsome. Having decided that his straight dark hair looked better curled, he spent time each day at the court hairdresser's, having it waved with heated tongs. "If I didn't have my hair curled every day I couldn't enjoy my food," he explained. He was self-conscious about his large ears, and grew his hair longer in an effort to de-emphasize them.

With each passing year, Ludwig retreated deeper into the fantasy world he created in his imagination. He preferred this place, full of legendary German heroes, to the real world whose people he found unpredictable. Throughout his life, he expressed hatred for the times he lived in. Always, he longed for the past and wished he could have lived during the historical time of knights and chivalry.

His childhood teacher, Fräulein Meilhaus, had married and become Baroness Leonrod. She attended a performance of German composer Richard Wagner's opera *Lohengrin* and immediately knew that her former pupil would love the medieval spectacle. She wrote to Ludwig, urging him to see a performance.

The prince's parents said no. Neither of them were opera fans, nor were they fond of Richard Wagner. Wagner was famous throughout Europe, but conservative Bavaria considered him notorious. Religious leaders disliked his scorn for established religion. Many musicians were jealous of his success, feeling that his music was overrated, too emotional, and over-the-top. The aristocracy condemned his revolutionary ideas. Wagner was never afraid to participate in public protests of any government policy with which he disagreed.

Additionally, Ludwig's parents thought that the twelve-year-old was too young and impressionable to see such an emotionally charged performance.

Ludwig bided his time, and three years later he was finally allowed to attend a performance of *Lohengrin*. As the fifteen-year-old prince entered the royal box at the court theater in the Residenz, the royal family's Munich palace, he had no idea how the next few hours would change his life.

Cushioned in his plush chair and separated from the masses, Ludwig was able to peer out from the velvet curtains and see characters from the Hohenschwangau murals actually come to life.

On stage, medieval Princess Elsa was falsely accused of murdering her brother. She prays for a defender, and who should arrive but the knight Lohengrin! Clad in shining armor, he floats serenely into the picture in a boat drawn by a swan. He challenges Elsa's accuser to a battle and defeats him, restoring Elsa's honor. Lohengrin declares his plans to marry Elsa and rule over the people, but only if they never ask his name or his history. Elsa is unable to overcome her curiosity and asks Lohengrin about his identity.

By now, Ludwig was leaning forward, on the edge of his seat. The soaring music, the operatic voices, and the dramatic stage sets filled him with delight. This was his dream world come true! What would happen to Elsa and Lohengrin?

Alas, Elsa's question had broken the spell and Lohengrin was forced to leave. But first, he told Elsa his name and revealed that his father was Parsifal, the king of the Temple of the Holy Grail. He was a god, and therefore his relationship with a human was doomed from the beginning.

Ludwig pondered this message. As future king, Ludwig knew he was a special messenger of God. Was this why human relationships were so difficult for him? It seemed reasonable to the prince. He was absolutely moved by Wagner's opera, and determined to see more.

The next year, Ludwig was able to fulfill this wish when he watched a performance of *Tannhäuser*, another medieval tale based on ancient German legend. The knight Tannhäuser falls in love with the beautiful princess Elizabeth. However, he also loves Venus, a goddess who lives in a grotto beneath the castle. Which will he choose?

As the music soared and Tannhäuser struggled to make his decision, the court secretary who accompanied Ludwig to the performance noted the prince's strong reaction to the opera. He noted that Ludwig "was thrown into such convulsions that I was afraid he might have an epileptic seizure." Seeing his heroes brought to life was almost more than Ludwig could bear, although he continued to watch Wagner's operas as often as possible. They allowed him to live through others in a way that he found impossible to do in his own interactions. They showed a world he loved, full of holy and pure heroes.

Ludwig had found a fragile balance in life. He was happy attending operas, gazing at the Hohenschwangau murals, becoming absorbed in books, riding in the mountains, and retreating from other humans as much as possible. Perhaps, he thought, he could live this way for many years.

Then, when Ludwig was eighteen, King Maximilian died.

Chapter 4

Ludwig's coronation portrait

"Called Too Young"

March, 1864: The United States was in the midst of the Civil War, pitting North against South. President Abraham Lincoln had just appointed General Ulysses S. Grant commander of all Union armies. Tension gripped the nation as it struggled to survive, with brother fighting against brother.

Across the Atlantic in Munich, the House of Wittelsbach faced its own troubles. Ludwig paced the hallways outside his father's bedroom at the Residenz. He was unable to sit hour after hour by the bedside, as his mother and Otto were doing. How could the king be on his deathbed? It was true that Maximilian had always been nervous and sickly. He had angered some Bavarians when he traveled to Italy in an effort to improve his health. But Max's doctors had said he was merely exhausted just a few weeks ago. Then he had developed a cold, and that led to pneumonia, and now, at just fifty-two, he was dying? This could not be!

The prince studied the heavy brocade drapes and the gilding along the walls. He loved the rich furnishings of his Munich home, though at nearly five hundred rooms covering several acres, the Residenz was hardly as cozy as Hohenschwangau. Still, its richness inspired him and helped distract him from his current distress. He loved to wander its halls, imagining he was back in the times of the French Bourbon kings. Surely, he would have felt more at home in the days of Marie Antoinette, when royal figures were revered as they should be. The growing egalitarian attitudes of the current day offended the prince.

In the dark early morning hours of March 10, 1864, the king called Ludwig in to his room. Years earlier, Max had said of Ludwig, "I have nothing in common with this young gentleman." But now, he knew that Ludwig would soon rule in his place. Max spoke his last words: "My son, when your time comes, may you die as peacefully as your father." Could Max have had an intuitive glimpse of Ludwig's sad departure from the world?

With his wife and sons close by, the king died a few hours later. He had ruled Bavaria for sixteen years, and had been a noted patron of science, law, art, music, and medicine. Although Ludwig had feared and disliked Max, he was by no means happy about his father's death. It meant that Ludwig would have to grow up quickly, for he was now King of Bavaria.

Overwhelmed with grief and fear regarding the future, Ludwig walked from his father's room. The adjoining halls were filled with whispering members of the court and royal household, but the quiet buzz stopped abruptly when Ludwig emerged. Every eye was on him.

A page bowed low and stammered, "Your Majesty!"

Ludwig shuddered.

Thankfully, Bavaria required no lavish Coronation ceremony for its king. Instead, Ludwig was officially named king at an accession council held at the Residenz two days later. To Baroness Leonrod, he wrote, "I carry my heart to the Throne – a heart which beats for my people and which glows for their welfare – all Bavarians may be assured of that. I will do everything in my power to make my people happy; their welfare, their peace are the conditions of my own happiness."

On March 14, Maximilian was buried in Munich's Theatiner Kirche. Ludwig and Otto walked behind the casket down the streets of Munich in the funeral procession, marking the first time most Bavarians had seen their new king. To say they were pleased would be an understatement.

Ludwig was quite tall at 6'4", and his ivory skin made a striking contrast to his dark, wavy hair and piercing blue eyes. His hours of riding and hiking had produced a fit, athletic physique.

"He was the most beautiful youth I have ever seen … even if he had been a beggar, I would have noticed him. Nobody, old or young, rich or poor, could have been left untouched by the charm which radiated from his personality," enthused an Austrian writer. German poet Paul Heyse commented, "The look in his beautiful, shining eyes was free and unselfconscious. He possessed an exceptionally sure knowledge of human nature which is remarkable considering that he had been brought up so alone and far from the world."

The crowds' calls, "The King is dead – long live King Ludwig!" unnerved the sensitive young monarch, who said, "It has been my fate to be called too young to face heavy responsibilities, too heavy for young shoulders, too difficult for a young brain, full till now of quite other thoughts and desires."

Ludwig's grandfather, Ludwig I, was still living. He sympathized with his grandson, writing to him, "In difficult times you succeed to the Throne too early."

Some of those closest to Ludwig feared for the future of both Bavaria and the new king. Ludwig's former teacher, de la Rosee, commented that Max's premature death was the worst possible tragedy which could have befallen Bavaria.

CHAPTER 5

Elisabeth (Sisi), Empress of Austria and Ludwig's cousin

THE GREAT FRIEND AND THE DOVE

Riding through the Bavarian mountains near Hohenschwangau on horseback, Ludwig was just where he wanted to be: alone, except for the groom trailing him. He entertained himself with his own thoughts, although these were not happy. He had been King of Bavaria for almost a month. Kings dealt with wars and treaties and laws. Kings needed to meet with their subjects. They had to attend endless meetings and councils. None of this interested Ludwig. In fact, it horrified him. How he wished he had been born during medieval times! He dreamed of being a chivalrous hero like the Swan Knight Lohengrin.

The king's mind wandered to his grandfather's reign. Ludwig I had remade Munich with his striking architectural creations. His recently deceased father had left a legacy by supporting Bavarian artists who had painted the haunting murals at Hohenschwangau. Ludwig pulled his horse to a stop and gazed over the serene Schwansee. Perhaps he could leave a mark as king in a way that he actually enjoyed. What could that be?

Ludwig recalled his sheer joy at watching the performances of *Lohengrin* and *Tannhäuser*. "Oh, really, one of the greatest enjoyments of the mind is to be carried away by these wonderful works – and then, elevated and strengthened, one can face the realities of life again," he had written to Baroness Leonrod. Ludwig couldn't imagine any gift he would rather give his people than the rapture of watching "wonderful works" like these. Leaving his poor groom struggling to keep pace, Ludwig galloped away with this triumphant thought: his lasting legacy as king would involve promoting the composer Richard Wagner!

Back home, Ludwig wrote a letter to Wagner, professing his admiration and inviting the composer to meet him. As a token of his respect, Ludwig added a silver framed photo of himself and a ruby ring, bearing the message: "As this stone burns, so do I burn with ardor to behold the creator of the words and music of *Lohengrin*." He gave these to his cabinet secretary with instructions to deliver them to Wagner.

The secretary was a bit puzzled by this. Why was the dashing eighteen-year-old king so taken with a fifty-year-old composer? There was also the issue of Wagner's location – no one was sure where to find him. He had lived as a nomad in recent years, moving from country to country in an attempt to escape his creditors. Although he had earned a decent living from his compositions, Wagner had extravagant tastes and spent money freely. He insisted on devoting all his mental energies to composing, and he demanded plush surroundings in order to do his best work.

Wagner had recently written to a fellow artist, "Some friend must arise to help me, who will take my part ... only a miracle can help me now, and that right soon, or I am done for!"

Fortunately for Richard Wagner, that miracle was about to occur.

Ludwig's cabinet secretary finally located the composer in the Bavarian city of Stuttgart, where he presented him with the king's letter and gifts.

Hardly believing this stroke of fortune, Wagner hurried back to Munich to meet the young king. How incredible that Ludwig, who had been born while Wagner was working on the lyrics to *Lohengrin*, should now become his savior!

The king and the composer met in a flurry of excitement, embracing each other rapturously. Physically, the two could not have made more of a contrast. The composer's short stature and large head looked almost comical next to the king's tall, athletic frame. But the men paid no attention to these differences. Each was ecstatic for different reasons. Ludwig was thrilled to meet the man who had brought his favorite tales to life, and Wagner was overjoyed to see his financial problems end. "I have no other disciple who is so utterly my own," Wagner wrote to a friend. "It is scarcely believable."

Meeting his idol did nothing to dampen the king's affection for the composer. An observer noted that Ludwig seemed "like a child who is waiting outside the room where the Christmas presents are being put out," when he met Wagner. Ludwig took his admiration a step further, expressing disbelief that anyone could fail to be so impressed: "Do you really believe it possible that the composer of *Lohengrin* has enemies?" he wondered. "It is unthinkable!"

The two men found they had much in common: both were romantics and were idealistic. On a less appealing note, they were both also egotists who thought highly of themselves. Each lived life largely for his own benefit.

Ludwig immediately commissioned a portrait of Wagner to be painted for the king's quarters. He also ordered a bust of the composer, which he planned to place in his study between those of Shakespeare and Beethoven. Did Ludwig, perhaps, idolize Wagner as the devoted father he never had?

After spending five days together, the king and "the Great Friend," as Ludwig dubbed Wagner, parted. But not for long. Anxious to keep Wagner nearby, Ludwig rented a house for him on the banks of Lake Starnberg. Berg, one of the smaller Wittelsbachs castles, lay on the same lake, just three miles away. Ludwig was less fond of Berg than Hohenschwangau, but his mother spent most of her time at Hohenschwangau, and the king avoided his mother whenever possible.

With the Great Friend so close, Ludwig spent much of the summer at Berg. Occasionally he and Wagner visited, but Ludwig wanted the composer to devote his days to creating glorious works. The two communicated mainly through letters, which became a type of reality for Ludwig. In person, he often had little to say. But given a pen and paper, the king became flowery and poetic. An example of a letter he wrote to Wagner shows just how excessive Ludwig could be:

> *My Heart's rapture gives me no peace; I must write to you. Nearer and nearer draws the happy day – Tristan will arise! … We must break through the barriers of custom, shatter the laws of the base, egotistical world. The ideal must and shall come to life. We will march forward conscious of victory. My loved one, I shall never forget you … My love for you and for your art grows ever greater and this flame of love shall bring you happiness and salvation. Oh – write to me – I yearn for it!*
>
> *Until death,*
>
> *Your faithful,*
>
> *Ludwig.*

Although largely solitary and reclusive, Ludwig did have a few close friends. One lifelong friend and soul mate was his cousin, Elisabeth, known as Sisi.

Sisi was another example of Wittelsbach eccentricity. Her parents were cousins, and at sixteen, she was married to her own cousin, twenty-three-year-old Emperor Franz Joseph of Austria.

Charming and attractive, Sisi was widely considered the most beautiful woman in the world during the 1860s and 1870s. She starved herself throughout much of her life to maintain the twenty-inch waist she was so proud of.

Her long chestnut hair was her most admired feature. It reached her knees, and she wore it in eight thick braids, sometimes wound around her head like a crown. Every three days, she washed her hair in a mixture of eggs and brandy. Washing and drying all that hair took an entire day, and even on non-washing days, Sisi spent three hours setting her hair.

Even Sisi's mother-in-law, who was not especially fond of her, could not deny that Sisi was "as lovely as an angel." Sisi worked hard to maintain her beauty, drinking several raw eggs daily because she felt that this enhanced her appearance. She washed her face with olive oil and went through a series of exercises each day on bars and rings installed in her home – the 1800s version of a "home gym." Sisi's only imperfections were her ugly yellow teeth. She tried to hide them by rarely opening her mouth when smiling, and by opening it only slightly when speaking. As you can imagine, she was often hard to understand!

Eight years older than her cousin Ludwig, Sisi and the king were not close as children. But once Ludwig became king, the pair spent much time together. Beautiful, older, and unattainable, Sisi was Ludwig's ideal woman.

The two understood each other well. Each was unsociable, extravagant, and melancholy in outlook. They each felt misunderstood and neither enjoyed royal duties. They both loved horseback riding, poetry, and taking long walks. Sisi understood and shared many of Ludwig's unusual behaviors, and she accepted him as he was. The king appreciated this, since many of his advisers and cabinet members made fun of him behind his back. Sisi was also one of the few whose relationship with Ludwig allowed for her to tease the serious king. She once laughed at him when she saw him dressed in full military uniform, carrying his helmet in one hand and an open umbrella in the other. "I've no intention of spoiling my hair," he snapped at her.

Ludwig idolized Sisi and frequently sent her flowers as a way of showing his love for her and his appreciation of her acceptance. Even when he refused to see government officials or pretended illness in order to miss an important meeting, Ludwig would make time to take long walks with Sisi or write her letters.

"I know that sometimes I am considered mad," Sisi once declared to a staff member. But while accusations of insanity troubled Ludwig, Sisi almost took pride in them, proclaiming, "I can do what I like!" and proceeding to do just that. So what if she insisted on traveling with a favorite cow so that she could drink the milk she wanted? She was Empress!

Ludwig admired his cousin's confidence. "I think that those who are taken to be insane are the only really intelligent people," Sisi wrote to him.

In letters, Ludwig always referred to Sisi as "the Dove" and himself as "the Eagle." This was his way of giving their relationship a pure, otherworldly feel. To the very end – and perhaps even beyond – Sisi and Ludwig retained their bond.

CHAPTER 6

Richard Wagner

TROUBLE BREWING

Settling into his role as king, Ludwig enjoyed the summer. Wagner was nearby, and the king loved the composer's updates on the new opera he was composing, *Tristan and Isolde*.

Wagner also composed a march to commemorate Ludwig's nineteenth birthday. The Great Friend arranged for a band of eighty musicians to assemble at Hohenschwangau on August 25. There, they would serenade the king with the first performance of the special birthday composition.

Ludwig was excited about this, but when his mother arrived at Hohen-schwangau, his enthusiasm vanished. "Unfortunately, my present stay is completely spoilt by Mother, who tortures me with her endless love; she has no idea of the rest and every sparkle of poetry vanishes in her company," he wrote. Ludwig canceled the performance.

But Ludwig's love of Wagner remained. He and the composer hatched a plan to build an extravagant theater in Munich where Wagner's works could be performed in a worthy setting. Treasury officials ended that dream when they refused to pay for the project. They were accustomed to Ludwig's father, King Maximilian, who had been frugal with Bavarian funds. Both Ludwig and Wagner were furious at this reversal, with Ludwig going so far as to quote Jesus' words in a letter to the composer: "Forgive them, for they know not what they do: they do not realize that for me you mean everything, now and until my dying day. How hard they make life for us! But I will not complain for I still have you, my Friend, my only friend."

The Bavarian people felt apprehensive about the relationship between their king and Richard Wagner. The newspaper reported all the perks the king was providing for the composer, including an annual spending allowance as well as the use of houses on Lake Starnberg and in Munich. Creditors all over Europe wanted Wagner to pay bills he had racked up for food, furniture, and more. Why, Bavarians wondered, should they finance his lavish lifestyle? The short, middle-aged man looked almost comical as he walked the streets of Munich. He was not remotely beautiful or appealing, as their young king was.

Public opinion of Wagner improved briefly when *Tristan and Isolde* premiered in Munich in June 1865. Wagner had been in Munich for a year at this point, and the opera's production was due to Ludwig's generous support. No one was more affected by the performance than the king. As he watched the tragic tale involving the typical Wagnerian love triangle, heroic themes, and larger-than-life heroes who can find fulfillment only in death, Ludwig gripped the edge of the royal box. Tears streamed down his face as he took on the emotions of the characters.

Even on the way home from the performance, the king remained agitated. He asked the royal train to stop while he got out and wandered the nearby forests for hours, trying to process the feelings the opera had stirred. Only when the sun began to rise did he return to his train and continue home.

But while Ludwig persisted in his opinion of Wagner as "a great and noble spirit – unfortunately not nearly so much appreciated as he deserves," the Bavarian people quickly returned to their disdain for the composer.

Royal officials grew increasing concerned that Wagner was taking up too much of the king's time. They noted that since the composer had come to Munich, Ludwig had held no court events – no balls, no banquets, no speeches. It seemed that he was living more and more in the fantasy world he had created, based largely on Wagner's operas. Ludwig countered that his isolation was his own choice, through no influence of Wagner's: "More than anything else I like to be alone."

Bavarian religious leaders, who were mostly Catholic, disliked Wagner's liberal Protestant influence. He had participated in riots in Dresden aimed at overthrowing the government. In fact, he had earned a reputation for stirring up trouble wherever he lived.

Wagner was aware of his unpopularity in Bavaria. He tried to convince Ludwig to replace officials hostile to himself with ones Wagner chose. But, although Ludwig put up with lies, snubs, and greed from Wagner (he would not have tolerated these from anyone else), he drew the line here. Ludwig was absolutely adamant about his power and authority as king. He had been taught from his earliest days that God had appointed him king! When Wagner started talking politics around the king, Ludwig looked up at the ceiling and began whistling to himself. He would not be forced to take advice from anyone else, not even the Great Friend.

Tensions in Munich continued to grow. The prime minister threatened to resign unless Richard Wagner left Bavaria. Ludwig and his mother attended a theater performance, and instead of their usual greeting of applause from the audience, they were hissed at. This upset the queen mother so much that she fainted and had to be carried out. Ludwig was distraught. How could things have deteriorated so much in the year and a half that Wagner had been in Bavaria?

Whispers throughout the land spread the notion that the Lola Montez scandal was happening all over again. Ludwig's grandfather, Ludwig I, had been forced to abdicate over the time and money he gave to the dancer. Now, his grandson appeared to be facing the same fate over time and money given to Richard Wagner.

As much as he loved Wagner, Ludwig would not let the composer force him from the throne. He sent a minor secretary, Johann von Lutz, to tell Wagner that he was being exiled from Bavaria.

Wagner left for Switzerland the next day. The king expected this to end the hostilities toward the composer, and hoped he would be able to return to Bavaria within a few weeks, or months at the longest.

Richard Wagner remained in Switzerland for six years.

Wagner once wrote, "The young king is unfortunately so handsome, a man of such fine sensibilities and splendid character that I fear his life is doomed to fade like a daydream at the first contact with this cruel world."

With Wagner gone, Ludwig soon faced that contact.

Ludwig's role as Bavarian king wasn't one that involved ruling the state on a daily basis. The role was similar to England's king: the monarch was consulted on all major issues, but didn't make the final decisions. The cabinet secretary was actually more powerful in running Bavaria. The state couldn't function without the cabinet secretary, but it could function without a king. Ludwig used this as an excuse to avoid government matters many times, but his distance from state affairs would eventually come to haunt him.

The modern country of Germany did not exist in Ludwig's day. Instead, the area consisted of around 300 different states which frequently fought each other. The largest and most powerful state was Prussia, located in what is now northern Germany. In 1862, Otto von Bismarck became chancellor of Prussia. Bismarck was shrewd, arrogant, and ambitious to expand Prussia's domination of the German states (and Europe as well).

Bavaria was the largest of the southern states. Austria controlled the northern state of Holstein, while Prussia controlled its neighbor, Schleswig. Bismarck wasn't happy with this arrangement, and in 1866 war threatened between Prussia and Austria.

Instead of considering Bavaria's options, Ludwig tried to ignore the whole thing. "I am sick of this eternal Schleswig-Holstein business ... Please don't show this to anybody!" he wrote to a friend.

Eventually, the king had to decide whether Bavaria would support Austria or Prussia in the hostilities. Although his patriotism for the German states was strong, Ludwig followed his ministers' advice to support Austria if war broke out.

Following this decision, Ludwig was overcome with depression. He had spent half of the previous year away from Munich, in his castles at Berg and Hohenschwangau. His subjects had begun referring to him as the "Fairy King" because of his love for the outdoors and remote locations. To be called back to the capital to make decisions so distasteful to him was almost more than his sensitive spirit could bear. War was ugly. He knew his troops would face injuries and death, and unlike Wagner's operas, there would be no knights in armor ... no soaring music or beautiful costumes to serve as a counterbalance.

Hostilities eventually reached the point where government officials advised the king to mobilize his army, and Ludwig called an emergency cabinet meeting. But instead of announcing a call to arms, he announced that he was abdicating the throne to his brother, Otto.

Leaving the cabinet to discuss this stunning news, Ludwig traveled to Berg. Lake Starnberg featured an isolated island called the Isle of Roses, and Ludwig often rowed there when he wanted to be alone. He went there now, and composed a letter to Wagner, telling him of his plans to give up the throne.

Wagner was horrified by this news. The composer's chief interest in Ludwig was the money he could provide, and Ludwig without a throne meant Ludwig without money. Wagner wrote back, urging the king to reconsider. "Denounce, I beseech you, during this half year, all concern with art and our plans … turn your attention with the greatest energy to affairs of state; give up your comfortable solitude in Berg; remain in your Residenz, stay with your people, show yourself to them. If you love me, as I have earnestly hoped, then hear my pleas."

On May 22, Ludwig was scheduled to open Parliament. He declined, telling aides that he was sick. Later in the day, concern grew when no one was able to locate the king. He was eventually found in Switzerland, where he had traveled to get away from the distasteful situation in Munich. He was with the Great Friend, celebrating Wagner's birthday.

The Bavarian newspaper condemned what it saw as a dereliction of duty by its king. Even Sisi, normally an ardent supporter, spoke disparagingly of her cousin: "I hear the King is away again," she wrote to her mother. "I wish he would care a little more about his duties, especially now when times are so bad."

Ludwig returned to Munich five days later, and was appalled when residents greeted him in the street with hisses. He put his discomfort aside and walked "like a young god" through the streets in a parade.

When war finally did break out in June, messengers traveled to Berg to inform Ludwig that Prussia had declared war on Austria, and therefore on Bavaria as well. Ludwig, in typical form, had instructed his guard to block the entrance and not allow the messengers in. The delegation passed along word to the prime minister. Furious at the king, the prime minister traveled to Berg. There he discovered Ludwig and a friend dressed in costumes from the opera *Lohengrin*, reciting poetry to each other.

Throughout the war, Ludwig avoided any news relating to the hostilities. He spent much time on the Isle of Roses, setting off fireworks. Members of Parliament sent to give him messages were often refused – "a case unparalleled in the Constitutional life of Bavaria," an aide wrote. The Austrian ambassador added, "One begins to think that the King is demented."

The prime minister wasn't the only one troubled by Ludwig's lack of interest in ruling his land. Especially in wartime, the Bavarian people looked to their king to draw them together and hope for better times. Instead, Ludwig tried to ignore the war, hoping that his disinterest might make it disappear. He refused the traditional role of commanding his troops, choosing instead to give that role to his seventy-one-year-old uncle, Prince Karl ("Prince Karl is too old to be Commander in Chief," wrote one advisor to another). Ludwig even declined requests to visit his troops, despite urging from Wagner: "Listen to me! … Fate calls: to the army!"

A few weeks into fighting, Ludwig gave in to pressure from officials, one of whom had noted, "If the King can ride for eight to ten hours in mist and darkness without endangering his health, then His Majesty is also able to devote a few hours to his Army." Reluctantly, he visited field headquarters. Walking slowly among the soldiers, many of them wounded, Ludwig was deeply traumatized by the effects of war he witnessed.

The soldiers had a different view of the visit of this "glorious figure." "He was so beautiful that my heart stopped beating," recalled one officer who saw him. "I was so deeply moved that a terrible thought seized me: this godlike youth is too beautiful for this world."

The Seven Weeks' War was thankfully brief. Prussia defeated Austria and Bavaria, which was no surprise because of the large and powerful Prussian army. Bismarck unified the northern states into a North German Confederation, and Austria was expelled from the German Union. Bavaria got off relatively easily, losing just a small amount of land and agreeing to pay a sum to Prussia. Bavaria also was forced to agree to support Prussia in future military campaigns.

The conflict crushed Ludwig's spirit. He hated the idea of war, with its ugliness and suffering. He saw no grand themes or redemption in fighting. He also saw that the war had eroded his power as king. Bismarck was turning Prussia into a powerful force, and he had to acknowledge its supremacy. How long could Bavaria hope to hold its own with nearby Prussia always hungry for more?

CHAPTER 7

Kőnig Ludwig II. mit feiner Braut Herzogin Sophie in Bayern
Photographifche Aufnahme von Jofeph Albert (1867)

Sophie and Ludwig's engagement photo

HAPPILY EVER AFTER?

Ludwig could not settle his nerves. The war had ended, but he was still troubled by images of wounded soldiers, and by the idea that Bavaria had sided against Prussia, another German state. The king decided to put his dislike of royal duty and his distaste for being stared at behind him. He would tour his country, and meet his people! He was the Lord's anointed, and he would show himself to his Bavarian subjects!

He embarked on his first (and last) tour of the state. The results were spectacular. Everywhere he went, Ludwig was greeted with affection and enthusiasm. The newspapers raved over his tall, dark, handsome appearance. Troops burst into applause when he appeared in village parades.

Ludwig overcame his shyness and showed his love for his subjects, taking remarkable interest in the details of their lives. He laid wreaths on the graves of those killed in battle. He provided dowries for young couples short of money, and sent medicines and his own doctor to some sick elderly subjects. He did not normally choose social interaction, but when it was forced upon him, he showed himself to be a compassionate leader.

The charming king enchanted his subjects. He made a particular impression on the young ladies, who showed their admiration by plucking up flowers the king had stepped on during parade routes to savor as keepsakes. Others clipped bits of hair from the royal horse as something by which to remember the handsome king. Ludwig was now twenty-one, and his subjects speculated wildly on when he would marry. They felt sure that a royal wedding would soon occur. Their only question was, who would the lucky young woman be?

Richard Wagner was eager for Ludwig to marry as well. The king's earlier threat to abdicate had frightened the composer, who felt that marriage would settle the king and therefore ensure Wagner's continuing income. He asked Ludwig for his idea of the ideal woman, and the king replied, "a beautiful soul in a beautiful dress with a voice like music and perfumed with lilies."

But Ludwig showed little interest in finding a wife. He told one government official, "I haven't time to get married – Otto can see to that." He held impossibly high standards for women, based on the ones he knew from Wagner's operas or from German folklore. Most were angels, goddesses or princesses, beautiful and pure. Since Ludwig had had very little interaction with girls or women, he was awkward in their presence.

One day, Ludwig visited his cousin Sisi at Possenhofen, her family's summer home on Lake Starnberg. He took note of her nineteen-year-old sister, Sophie. The king had hardly noticed Sophie before, but with growing speculation about his romantic life, he gave her a second look. She was lovely, sensitive, and pale. Perhaps her personality was similar to her sister's, which Ludwig adored. He visited Sophie several times, although the two rarely talked. Ludwig preferred to sit silently and listen to Sophie play and sing songs by Wagner.

At a Court Ball, Sophie wore a shimmering satin and velvet silver gown made in Paris, adorned with her mother's jewels. Ludwig, who normally despised such events, was mesmerized by Sophie's beauty on this night. Perhaps she was the real-life angel for him?

A week later, everything changed for Sophie and Ludwig. Both attended the Officers' Ball, and Sophie was awarded a prize for beauty. This heightened Ludwig's interest. "Many lovely women were there, but none so beautiful as my cousin Sophie!" he proclaimed. The two made a beautiful couple, with Ludwig in a dashing blue military uniform and Sophie in another flowing gown. They danced together for the rest of the night.

Ludwig spent several hours alone that night after returning home, thinking of Sophie. As was his pattern, he created a character in his mind and then assumed that Sophie would match the ideal he imagined. He grew more and more taken with the perfect woman he had created, and his emotions became stronger and stronger. He felt just as moved as he would when watching a Wagner opera, only this was real life! The king flew down the stairs as the sun rose, asking his mother to go along with him to propose to Sophie.

The Queen Mother was thrilled that her son was interested in marrying such a sweet girl, and a relative besides! The two hurried to Possenhofen, surprising Sophie and her family, who had just sat down to breakfast.

Sophie and her family were delighted. Her parents were excited that their daughter would be Queen one day, and Sisi was happy to further cement her friendship with Ludwig by becoming his sister-in-law as well as his cousin. Indeed, Ludwig once told Sisi (in front of Sophie) that his favorite thing about his fiancée was her resemblance to her older sister.

Of Sophie's thoughts we know little, although we can assume that most any young woman of the day would be thrilled to find herself engaged to a king who was by all accounts quite a catch. Handsome, dark, moody and brooding, Ludwig had a lot in common with Mr. Rochester (you'll have to read *Jane Eyre* to understand).

An engagement photo shows Sophie arm in arm with her fiancé, a serious expression on her face. Ludwig stares off into the distance, hardly looking like a smitten suitor.

The night of the engagement, January 22, 1867, Ludwig and his mother attended a performance at the court theater. During intermission, the two walked to Sophie's seat in her father's box and escorted her to the king's box. Gossip in the audience reached fever pitch: did this signal that an engagement announcement was imminent?

A week later, the engagement was officially announced, breaking the hearts of young women all over Bavaria. Most of the country, however, was ecstatic. They would be getting a Bavarian princess, not the Prussian one many had feared.

Ludwig I was thrilled to see his grandson settling down. It appeared that his reign would be less tumultuous than Ludwig I's had been: "May God's blessing, dear Ludwig, rest upon your marriage! I have for some time read in the looks of the beautiful Sophie that you are deep-rooted in her heart … Happiness at home is the greatest blessing on earth. How happy I shall be to carry your first son, my great-grandson, in my arms!"

Richard Wagner breathed a sigh of relief as well. But did he find it odd that Ludwig wrote of his engagement by saying, "Walther confirms to the dear Sachs that he has found his faithful Eva – Siegfried his Brunhilde," calling everyone by names from Wagner's operas? Wagner likely dismissed this as Ludwig being Ludwig.

Even as the engagement was announced, there were warning signs that not all was well. Ludwig declared, "My love for [Sophie] is deep and loyal;

but The Friend will never cease to be dear to me beyond all others." At an official engagement ball honoring the couple, Ludwig excused himself early and left, without even letting Sophie know he was going. His destination? The final act of an opera performance. He hurried away into the night, no doubt hugely relieved that he could trade the hustle and bustle of the crowd for the happy seclusion of the royal box.

Whatever her reservations may have been, Sophie pushed them aside and threw herself into wedding plans. Ludwig took part as well, ordering an ornate golden state wedding coach (you can still see it, in all its splendor, in the Royal Stables Museum in Munich). Eight specially trained black horses were brought in to pull it. At the Residenz in Munich, the king had a suite of rooms furnished and decorated for Sophie. They were just beneath his rooms, and a small staircase was built to connect the two suites.

The wedding was planned for Ludwig's 22nd birthday, August 25, 1867. The festivities would last from 10:30 a.m. to 10 p.m., with a break from 3:00 until 6:00, and Ludwig described them to Sophie as "magnificent but terrible."

As the wedding approached, Ludwig retreated from specifics more and more. He had taken to calling Sophie "Elsa" in tribute to the *Lohengrin* heroine, and himself "Heinrich." Did Sophie find it odd when the subject of many letters from Ludwig was not their upcoming wedding, but Richard Wagner?

"Oh, I do wish you were here, beloved Elsa, I would come over so often …" Ludwig wrote. "Now, I think I will write to the precious distant one [Wagner]."

And the king wasn't content to just write about Wagner himself. He wanted Sophie to do the same! "My dear Elsa! Give me pleasure by writing very soon (perhaps tomorrow morning) to Wagner; I know how happy He will be to get a letter from you. And now, heartily good night! Your loving faithful Heinrich."

Sophie, like Ludwig, was a fan of Wagner's music – at least enough that she enjoyed singing and playing arias from his operas. But no doubt this extreme worship of the composer struck her as a bit odd. When Ludwig wrote to her, "The God of my life, as you know, is Richard Wagner," we can assume she felt a little dejected.

Ludwig didn't know when to quit. "Have you written to Wagner?" he asked Sophie. "Have you read his Autobiography?" And, as if to try to erase her identity even further, he wrote, "Very soon we shan't be any longer Sophie and Ludwig but Lohengrin and Elsa."

Although the engaged couple mainly communicated through letters, they did visit on occasion. Ludwig made surprise, spur-of-the-moment visits to Possenhofen. His nocturnal habits led him to often ride over from Berg at night, and his arrival startled the household. He always insisted that he be welcomed in a manner befitting his royal status, forcing the family to quickly awaken and dress to greet him.

Ludwig demanded to meet with Sophie alone on these visits, where he requested that Sophie sing and play Wagner's music while he mainly sat silently, listening. The two found they had little to say to each other, although Ludwig occasionally broke the silence with a comment complimenting Sophie's pretty eyes. The king was faced with the nagging impression that his fiancée was not as charming and intelligent as he had originally thought. When he was ready to leave, his habit was to kiss her on the forehead. After weeks of this, Sophie grew frustrated and pulled Ludwig toward her, kissing him on the lips. Shocked and horrified, the king came close to canceling the engagement then and there.

On another visit, Ludwig brought along a crown for Sophie to try on. It was too large, and the king collapsed in laughter as he watched his fiancée's attempts to put it on. Sophie wasn't nearly as amused, and cried, "He does not love me! He is merely playing with me!"

She was on to something. Ludwig's feet grew colder by the day. He imagined thousands of people lining the streets, watching the spectacle of this wedding that he was increasingly unsure of. He told one of his officials that he would rather drown himself in the Alpsee lake than go through with the wedding (a curious statement, in light of future events). A servant found him sitting at his dressing table one evening, making faces at himself in the mirror and saying, "At times, I would not swear that I am not mad."

But Ludwig had a strong sense of responsibility, and he was reluctant to break his engagement to Sophie. How could he get out of it? He asked his doctor, without success, to write a certificate declaring him unfit to marry.

Running out of time, the king postponed the wedding to October 12, claiming as the reason that this was the anniversary both of his parents and his grandparents.

An August performance of *Tannhäuser* prompted gossip when Ludwig sat alone in the royal box, while Sophie watched from her father's box. The public knew something must be amiss with the upcoming royal wedding.

Ludwig seemed to view the wedding as no longer being an issue in a letter he wrote to his beloved teacher, Baroness Leonrod: "The happy feeling which inspires me now that I have shaken off the burdensome bonds – which I knew would turn out unfortunate for me – can only be compared with the rapture of a convalescent who at last breathes again with the fresh air after a dangerous illness. Sophie was dear and precious to me as a friend and darling sister, but she would not have done for my wife; the nearer the date of the wedding came the more I dreaded my intended step. I felt very, very unhappy and so resolved to free myself from the self-imposed bonds and chains … I am still young and marriage would have been premature anyhow."

Perhaps the king hoped that his subjects would forget about the postponed wedding, but this was not the case. As the October date neared, Ludwig yet again postponed the wedding, this time to November 29.

Sophie's father had had enough of his indecisive future son-in-law. He wrote the king a letter, demanding that Ludwig set a firm wedding date or call it off altogether. Ludwig was thrilled. Here was his excuse! Immediately, he wrote to Sophie: "Beloved Elsa, Your Parents desire to break our engagement. I accept their proposal."

In his own diary, Ludwig's unfiltered relief was obvious. "Sophie got rid of. The gloomy picture fades. I longed for freedom, thirsted for freedom, to awake from this terrible nightmare! ... Thanks be to God, the fearful thing was not realized."

The king wasn't as cold-hearted as he sounds from the harsh note he wrote to inform his fiancée of the wedding cancellation. A few days later, he wrote her a long, heartfelt letter explaining his reasons for bowing out, and offering his friendship. He even suggested that the two could consider marrying again if she had not found a suitable husband candidate within the year. Sophie didn't take him up on that offer.

Ludwig did all he could to erase any reminders of Sophie and the wedding, from throwing a bust of her out the window and ordering commemorative wedding coins withdrawn from circulation to instructing that officials buy and smash all wedding vases and plates available in stores. Ludwig watched as servants, at his command, poured acid over copper plates made to celebrate the wedding that never was.

The Bavarian people were crushed and confused. Why had the wedding been canceled? Most placed the blame on Sophie. Rumors at the time suggested that she and court photographer Edgar Hanfstaengl, who had visited Possenhofen that year to take engagement photos of Sophie and Ludwig, had fallen in love. Letters from Sophie to Edgar were later found confirming this. "With horror I look upon the future, my wedding day stands like a black shadow before my soul - I want to flee from this merciless fate," Sophie wrote to Edgar in July 1867. "Why couldn't we meet before my freedom was taken from me? My Edgar, I love you so sincerely. When I am with you I find it difficult telling you how deeply I carry you in my heart. So deeply, I am slowly forgetting all duties towards my king."

But while mainstream Bavarians may have given the king a pass on the wedding fiasco, those who knew Ludwig well were less forgiving. The Russian Empress wrote, "I give [Ludwig] up, he really cannot be quite right in the head! I should like to hear what his mother has to say about it!"

Sisi, normally supportive of Ludwig in all things, drew the line when it came to her little sister. "You can well imagine how angry I am about the King, and so is the Emperor," she wrote. "There are no words for such behaviour. I cannot understand how he can show his face in Munich after all that has happened. I am glad that Sophie has taken it as well as she has. God knows that she could never have been happy with such a husband."

What became of Sophie? She and Edgar felt their future was doomed due to the different social worlds they inhabited. They parted, and the next year, 1868, Sophie married Prince Ferdinand d'Orleans, a grandson of French King Louis Philippe. As she walked down the aisle at Possenhofen to strains of *Lohengrin*, she didn't see Ludwig's face in the crowd. He was on the Isle of Roses in Lake Starnberg, not pining away after his lost love, but setting off fireworks. When the couple visited him later, he described himself as "bored to death."

Ludwig saw his escape from marriage as most would view an escape from death. He never again had a romantic relationship, or even a close friendship, with a woman.

CHAPTER 8

Ludwig's winter garden at the Residenz in Munich

"POETIC PLACES OF REFUGE"

The early years of Ludwig's reign had been anything but pleasant. He had brought the Great Friend, Wagner, to Bavaria, only to have him cast out. He had desired peace, only to see his country plunged into a war against his wishes. He had attempted to please his subjects with his engagement to Sophie, but that had ended in disaster. His sensitive spirit shattered, Ludwig realized he had little desire to live as his countrymen and officials wanted him to. From now on, he determined, he would live as he wanted to. He was the king! He could do anything he pleased!

Most of what pleased Ludwig involved architecture. However, his grandfather, Ludwig I, had already remade much of Munich architecturally. There was little for Ludwig to transform, but his interests centered around more

personal projects anyway. Having found much of the real world disappoint-
ing and distasteful, Ludwig lived through stage performances and books.
But, he wondered, what if he could create real-life versions of those performances and tales? Then he could actually see and walk among the scenes he
could now only imagine! "Oh, how necessary it is to create for oneself such
poetic places of refuge where one can forget for a little while the dreadful
times in which we live," Ludwig wrote to Baroness Leonrod.

The king's first venture into designing a fantasy world involved his bedroom
at Hohenschwangau. To complement the outdoor scenes in the room's
wall murals, Ludwig had the ceiling painted a nighttime shade of blue, and
added stars and even a moon that were illuminated by lighting lamps in the
room above. He brought in potted orange trees to add a lifelike feel to the
room, and installed a fountain as well.

Ludwig's next project was larger in scope: a winter garden at the Munich
Residenz. "Winter gardens" were popular during the 1800s as places where
people could experience the outdoors year-round, somewhat like grander
versions of today's sunrooms. Ludwig expanded the winter garden originally built by his father, Maximilian II, on part of the Residenz roof. It
was made of glass with an iron frame, based on the design of the Crystal
Palace built for the 1851 Great Exhibition in London (Disney World's Crystal Palace restaurant was inspired by the London Crystal Palace as well).

The curved glass roof reached a height of thirty-three feet, and the court
gardener filled the grounds with lush greenery, a large artificial pond, and
even a waterfall. Ludwig loved to stroll along the paths in solitude, watching
his beloved swans float past. On one occasion he requested a pair of gazelles
and a baby elephant for the garden as well. He hired Munich stage designer
Christian Jank to paint huge murals for the walls, which made the space
appear even larger. Several murals were completed, allowing Ludwig to
create the look he desired at a particular time. One depicted an Indian
palace; another, the Himalayan Mountains. An artificial sun and moon
hung in the sky.

Mostly, Ludwig used his winter garden as a place to escape from other people, but a fortunate few were invited in. One shared her impressions of the garden's magic: "We came to a door hidden by a curtain. With a smile the King drew aside the curtain. I could not believe my eyes. There, before us, was an enormous garden, illuminated in Venetian style, with palms, a lake, bridges, huts and castellated buildings. 'Come in,' said the King and I followed him, fascinated."

Many of the visitors Ludwig invited into the garden were actors whose opera performances he had enjoyed. The garden's romantic atmosphere overcame one of these actresses, a singer named Josefine Scheffsky. She and Ludwig were floating in a canoe in the winter garden pond, when Josefine managed to tip the boat over and began to shriek for Ludwig to save her. However, the king was merely annoyed at this inconvenience and rang a bell for a footman to come drag her out of the water. He was so unimpressed by Josefine's full figure that he requested that she stand behind large potted plants in the garden when she came up to sing for him, so he could hear her without having to look at her.

Reports of the magical garden on the rooftop spread among the Munich public, who often cast a glance skyward at night to gaze on the illuminated dome. Queen Marie's apartments were located just beneath the Winter Garden, and one night she awoke to a flood of water pouring through her ceiling. It seems that Ludwig's artificial moon had fallen into the pond, resulting in a flood. The cook's quarters were located beneath the Winter Garden as well, and Ludwig's cook reportedly took an umbrella to bed each night in case of leaking.

Ludwig I's death in 1868 at age eighty-one opened up new opportunities in his grandson's life. A quarter of Ludwig's annual civil list (basically his government salary) had gone to his grandfather as a pension. Another half of the money went to Ludwig II's various servants and relatives, leaving the king with only a quarter of the amount left. With his grandfather gone, that portion of the money was now available to Ludwig.

How to spend it? Ludwig stood at Hohenschwangau, gazing thoughtfully out over the Füssen plain with its rolling hills. Turning, he smiled and nodded at the Jugend Mountain. This Alpine peak had fascinated the king since childhood, when he had spent hours riding there and exploring the medieval ruins left on its crags. His mind had run wild with scenes of chivalry and pageantry as he imagined the knights on horseback who had lived there ages ago.

Now, with more funds available to him, Ludwig decided that he would build his first personal castle there. The spot was within sight of Hohenschwangau Castle, which he loved, but which was "profaned each year by the presence of my prosaic mother," as he wrote to Wagner.

Jugend Mountain was high and inaccessible, one of the settings of great natural beauty that Ludwig had such a talent for choosing. Here he imagined a fairy castle in the clouds, far from the interfering eyes of his subjects. He could reign there in isolation, living in the fantasy world he was sure he could create.

During the summer of 1868, Ludwig had an area on the mountain surveyed, and ordered the medieval ruins demolished. One year later, the dolomite foundation was completed. This was no small task, considering that the stone extended 165 feet into the mountain rock. Additionally, all materials for the mostly-limestone castle needed to be mined from a nearby quarry and carted up the mountain by horses. Still, Ludwig was spending his own money, and for almost two decades, Neuschwanstein Castle ("new swan castle") was the largest employer in the region, providing incomes for up to 300 workers during that time.

Ludwig again chose stage designer Christian Jank to help him create the castle of his dreams. It's not unusual that the king chose a theatrical expert rather than an architect, because his plan was to create a real-life set where he could live within scenes from his favorite German tales and Wagner operas.

Over the years, the gleaming white castle emerged from the mountain. Up close, it appeared even more spectacular. A red brick gatehouse with towers on each side led to a courtyard designed like the Munich stage set of *Lohengrin*, the opera which had introduced Ludwig to Wagner's work.

The courtyard was designed to hold a massive keep and a chapel, but these were never built. In fact, only fifteen of the castle's planned 200 rooms were finished. But the ones that were completed were breathtaking, an ode to German chivalry.

Neuschwanstein features dark wood paneling intricately carved, and of course the vibrantly colored murals Ludwig grew up loving. These murals depicted all his favorite tales of German heroism and mythical love. The king was intricately involved in all aspects of the castle, and was particularly concerned that the artwork be accurate in his estimation. He wrote to the artist who had painted a mural of *Lohengrin* at Neuschwanstein: "His Majesty wishes that in the new sketch the ship be placed further from the shore, that Lohengrin's neck be less tilted, that the chain from the ship to the swan be of gold and not of roses, and finally that the style of the castle shall be kept medieval."

Off of Ludwig's study, a door leads to an artificial cave. The cave, complete with stalactites and a fountain, is lit from above with hidden red, blue, and yellow lights. It was inspired – no surprise here – by a scene from *Tannhäuser*.

Ludwig's bedroom is a masterpiece of woodcarving, particularly his bed itself, which reportedly took 14 woodcarvers four years to complete. Its wood canopy extends up and up, featuring a forest of tiny soaring spires and pillars. Rich canopies in blue – Ludwig's favorite color – hang along the sides so the king could cocoon himself in total privacy. A washstand near the bed boasts a golden swan as a faucet, with water pouring from its mouth.

The castle's larger rooms defy description. The Singers' Hall, again modeled on a scene from a Wagner opera, takes up the entire fourth floor of the castle.

Murals line every wall, illustrating the story of the knight Parsifal. The huge golden chandeliers and golden candelabra lighting the room and its stage are an example of the excess seen in most of Ludwig's building projects. As he aged, the king's eyesight deteriorated. Yet he didn't like the way he looked in glasses, and refused to wear them. Instead, he ordered décor for his castles that featured ever-brighter colors, ever more gold and gilding, and ever-richer fabrics. To the average eyes, it was all too much. But to the king, it was perfect.

Neuschwanstein's crown jewel was the Throne Room, a two-story grand space intended to hold a throne that was never made. The mosaic floor features two million pieces of tile, arranged to depict various trees and animals. Paintings over the throne area show Jesus, his mother Mary, and angels, in a visual reminder that the king is God's appointed ruler. A huge golden chandelier holding 96 candles hangs over the space before the white marble steps leading up to the missing throne.

Soaring towers are plentiful at Neuschwanstein, with staircases curving around central columns that are carved with yet more mythical scenes. The columns are painted to show palm fronds bursting from the tops, and the blue ceilings are scattered with innumerable shining golden stars.

Ludwig was a Walt Disney ahead of his time, and he would have loved Disney's quote, "If you can dream it, you can achieve it." But his dreams were sometimes frustrated. He wanted to create one set of steps at Neuschwanstein with water rushing down the staircase, but his more practical-minded designer said no.

In addition to its many fanciful elements, Neuschwanstein was also a technological marvel of its day. Despite its medieval appearance, the castle was centrally heated with a hot air system. Its modern kitchen featured ducts beneath the floor to carry smoke from the oven to the chimney.

Ludwig adored his castle, but after all of his planning and efforts, Neuschwanstein was never completed. Richard Wagner never set foot in this shrine to his works. Ludwig himself ended up spending only 172 days there, and despite his pleasure over Neuschwanstein as a world of his own reality, an air of loneliness permeated its hallways. No queen, prince, or princess ever joined Ludwig in this fairy tale castle.

CHAPTER 9

Wilhelm I is crowned Emperor of Germany at Versailles

WAR, TAKE TWO

Much as he would have enjoyed spending the rest of his reign designing castles, real life intruded into Ludwig's world. After the Seven Weeks' War, Bavaria had signed an agreement to side with Prussia in future military conflicts. Ludwig no doubt hoped there would be no need to ever act on this agreement, but just four years later, in 1870, hostilities between France and Prussia escalated to the point where war was imminent.

Panicked, Ludwig tried to escape the situation. He hurried away to a remote hunting lodge in the mountains for several days, and when officials insisted that he return to civilization, he headed to his castle at Berg. This was still not ideal for reacting to quickly-changing events, because Ludwig often rowed out to the remote Isle of Roses to get away from his government ministers.

The king asked for a report on the pending crisis, and his cabinet secretary hurried over at midnight. Ludwig met with him for four hours, insisting on royal protocol, which demanded that the secretary stand the entire time he was in the king's presence. Ludwig, stressed to his limit, smoked cigarette after cigarette while listening.

"Is there no way, no possibility of avoiding war?" he asked repeatedly, highly distraught. Told that war was the only possible course of action, Ludwig buried his face in his hands.

The idea of opposing France didn't bother the king. While he loved the Bourbon period of French history, specifically the times of King Louis XIV, he had no affection for contemporary France. But Ludwig had always detested the brutality of war, no matter whom it was fought against.

The king considered declaring Bavaria neutral in the war. But, he feared that such an action would anger Prussia. Bavaria could lose her independence altogether, something Ludwig could not accept. Reluctantly, he signed an order mobilizing his troops.

Ludwig returned to Munich and was shocked at the overwhelming reception he received there. Everywhere, crowds cheered the announcement of war. When the king made a rare appearance from a window of the Residenz, he was cheered with shouts of "God save the King!"

Prussia defeated France in the brief conflict, known as the Franco-Prussian War. In similar fashion to his conduct during the Seven Weeks' War, Ludwig declined to direct his own troops, deferring leadership to two elderly generals. "He never accompanied his soldiers except on the piano," reported a French newspaper.

At the war's conclusion, the German states were reorganized into something close to modern-day Germany. Ludwig hoped that he, as head of the House of Wittelsbach, might be offered the Imperial Crown of Germany. After all, the Wittelsbachs were Europe's longest-ruling dynasty, ruling Bavaria since 1180. However, Prussian President Bismarck had not engaged in so many military quests in order to elevate Bavaria or Ludwig. Each military victory had increased Prussia's dominance in Europe, and now Bismarck intended nothing less than to unify Germany under Prussian control.

That's just what he did in forming the German states into the "Second Reich," or second kingdom. The First Reich had been the Holy Roman Empire that had existed from the ninth century until now. The Third Reich was the name later given by Adolph Hitler to his Nazi regime in Germany during World War II.

The leader of Imperial Germany was announced; it was to be Ludwig's uncle, Prussia's King Wilhelm. Ludwig was devastated. He saw his own power being greatly reduced. He refused to attend the post-war negotiations, even though they were held at one of his favorite locations, the Palace of Versailles in France. Again, he toyed with the idea of abdicating the throne. Ludwig decided to send his brother Otto to Versailles in his place.

However, Otto was no longer the warm, unassuming child both his parents had favored. At Versailles, he showed some of the first clear signs that he was not quite right. Others noticed the king's brother sitting silently through meetings, not speaking but shivering and staring vacantly into the distance.

Forced to sign a letter proclaiming his uncle Emperor of Germany, Ludwig saw the end of his sovereignty. He had come to the throne desiring absolute authority, yet during his years as king he had seen nothing but a constant erosion of his power. As was his pattern, Ludwig decided to retreat even further into isolation.

CHAPTER 10

Palace and grounds at Linderhof

LINDERHOF

The king was pleased with the progress on Neuschwanstein. The castle in the clouds fulfilled his desire to rule with absolute authority in the kingdom created in his mind. But the dark, gothic feel inside Neuschwanstein was just one aspect of Ludwig's mental landscape. An 1867 visit to the Palace of Versailles in France had brought the lifestyle of Kings Louis XIV, XV, and XVI to life for Ludwig. He loved the golden gilding everywhere, the opulence, and the aristocratic feel of the palace. Why not build his own version of Versailles?

Ludwig always had a great eye for location. Just as the Jugend Mountain had been an ideal setting for Neuschwanstein, the isolated Graswang Valley was perfect for his next creation, called Linderhof. The valley was less than twenty miles from Neuschwanstein, and once held a small hunting lodge belonging to Ludwig's father. Maximilian had often taken young Ludwig there, and the boy had been entranced by the magnificent views – the mountains contrasting with the vivid green of the trees. However, Ludwig quickly saw that the landscape was unsuitable for a copy of the grand Palace of Versailles.

Instead, the king looked for inspiration to the Grand Trianon, a smaller royal retreat on the grounds of Versailles. The result, built between 1870 and 1878, was Linderhof, named after the linden trees that grew in profusion in the area.

Ludwig took interest in every detail of Linderhof's construction. Realizing that his kingly powers mattered little in the affairs of Bavaria, he decided to compensate by exercising absolute authority in his building projects. He instructed trial walls to be erected so that he could visualize how his plans would look. He often changed his mind, and had certain areas torn down and rebuilt two or even three times before he was satisfied.

Linderhof has a totally different look and feel from Neuschwanstein. It was the castle where Ludwig spent more time than any other, and the only one of his three creations that he saw completed. Linderhof isn't really a "castle" at all, but more an aristocratic palace, smaller and more intimate than the king's other creations. It is often called a "jewel," and it's easy to see why when you gaze at it. Its ashlar stone gleams white, almost like a wedding cake, against the green valley surrounding it. The front, or façade, of Linderhof is full of Rococo carving (Rococo refers to a French style of art popular in the eighteenth century, featuring fussy and elaborate scrolls, leaves, and animals). Golden statues of cupids, spouting a spray of water almost a hundred feet high, rise from a pool in front of the palace.

Inside, there's no doubt that this isn't Neuschwanstein. Instead of deep, dark wood paneling and heavy murals, Ludwig chose gold, gold, and more gold for his palace celebrating Louis XIV, "The Sun King." Gilding is everywhere, as are carvings and paintings featuring scenes from the French court and countryside. Two carved and painted peacocks were placed in the marble entrance whenever Ludwig was in residence to announce his presence. Throughout his life, Ludwig identified strongly with both the swan and the peacock. Both animals appear frequently in his castles.

Ludwig's bedroom was a blinding vision, with gold everywhere. He had the room enlarged twice, so that it could adequately convey the glory of his royal presence. The room was lit by a 1000-pound crystal chandelier, and low gold fencing (called a balustrade) set apart the king's bed from the rest of the room, where courtiers could stand and conduct business with the king while he remained in bed. Louis XIV had done this, after all, and so Ludwig figured it was appropriate for him as well. The bedroom looks out on a magnificent series of thirty terraced marble steps, with water flowing over them into a pool complete with statues. In contrast to the sunny south-facing bedroom at Versailles, Ludwig's bedroom at Linderhof faces north. Perhaps Ludwig planned this to symbolize that he was the Moon King while the admired Louis XIV was the Sun King.

The dining room featured one of Ludwig's most famous idiosyncrasies: the Tishlein Deck Dich, or table that sets itself. The king liked to dine alone, saying "Solitary meals are far better than those taken … with people one dislikes." This table allowed him to do just that. When he was ready to dine, Ludwig pressed a switch and a mechanical device lowered the table to the kitchen below, where servants would fill it with sumptuous dishes and raise it up to him. When he had finished, another press of the switch sent his dishes back to the kitchen. This made it easy for the king to avoid the "gossiping servants" he so disliked.

A Hall of Mirrors created an illusion of infinity that the king loved. Mirrors on opposite walls reflected each other, resulting in the appearance of an immense, never-ending space.

Linderhof's main floor held just six rooms, plus a "cabinet" in each corner. These cabinets were small "waiting room" areas, and they were identical except for the colors of the silk adorning the walls and the furniture. One was rose, another mauve, one yellow, and the final one blue.

"I am going to build a little palace with a formal garden in the Renaissance style; the whole will breathe the magnificence and imposing grandeur of the Royal Palace at Versailles," Ludwig wrote to Baroness Leonrod, and in this he succeeded. The gardens surrounding Linderhof are vast, complemented with stairs, gazebos, and statues.

Ludwig designed the Linderhof estate with everything he could want. In addition to the palace, there were numerous other amusements fit for a king. One was his Moorish kiosk, an Indian pavilion he had purchased from the owner of a castle in Bohemia. Ludwig loved all things Asian. The outside of the pavilion featured a gleaming golden dome. Inside, there was a peacock throne where the king could relax while reading or simply gazing at the fountain in the center, or out of the stained-glass windows. Sometimes, Ludwig invited stable boys and other servants to the kiosk. The entire group sat cross-legged, dressed in Indian costumes and smoking Persian water pipes.

When Ludwig was in the mood to do a little play-acting, he could head to Hunding's Hut, in a wooded area. This large "hut" featured a stage set tree from the opening act of Wagner's opera *Die Walküre*, which Ludwig had first seen performed around the time Linderhof was begun, in 1870. Christian Jank, who designed the Munich stage set for the opera, designed this hut as well.

Not far from the hut, Ludwig chose an area thick with trees to construct a hermitage. This was a simple wooden thatched-roof building based, yet again, on a scene from a Wagner opera, this time *Parsifal*. One of the many quirks of Ludwig's personality was his ability to appreciate total opposites: elegant castles, and also the simplest of wooden huts. The king enjoyed coming here to read in quiet, and to feed hungry deer when winter storms had left them with little food. He made a tradition of visiting the hermitage each year on Good Friday. For this day, he insisted that a flowering meadow surround the hut. If flowers weren't currently in bloom, he instructed servants to plant some all around the building. The garden director carried out the king's wishes, a few times even when snow covered the ground.

Finally, when Ludwig desired a truly magical escape, he climbed to a clearing on the mountainside, and pressed a secret latch on a stone slab to reveal the Venus Grotto, a cavern complete with a lake and a waterfall. This was no small space. It was several hundred feet long and fifty feet high, made of iron girders and pillars covered with cement in order to look like a natural cave. Ludwig often rowed on the lake in a special boat shaped like a shell, floating among the lake's swans, which he fed with bread baked specially for them. An interior cave wall featured a painted scene from Wagner's opera *Tannhäuser*.

From the ceiling, flower garlands wove around stalactites. The whole atmosphere was given an eerie (or inspiring, depending on your perspective) feel by lights that changed from red to violet, and from rose to yellow. Despite his fairy tale image, Ludwig was quite up-to-date for his time, using state-of-the art technology here as he had at Neuschwanstein. One of Bavaria's first generators powered the lights, as well as the waves on the lake.

You might guess, correctly, that Ludwig planned to have *Tannhäuser* performed here, but criticism by the press and government officials prevented this from ever happening. However, the king did arrange for a few privileged actors and singers to perform for him in the grotto.

Ludwig could have lived out his life enjoying relaxing weekends at Linderhof after spending the week attending to royal duties in Munich. Unfortunately, his temperament made such a life impossible. The very things that brought the king joy were leading to his early demise.

Chapter 11

Ludwig on one of his nighttime sleigh rides

A Day in the Life

What did Ludwig's typical day hold – plans for war, blueprints for the next castle? Sometimes, but mostly his life was less eventful than might be expected from the king of one of Germany's largest states.

Let's take a look at Ludwig around 1874, when he had been on the throne for ten years. Physically, he had changed. He was no longer the handsome, dashing figure he had been in his youth. He was bloated and heavy. His love of sweets, along with his fear of visiting the dentist, had resulted in several lost teeth. Those that remained caused him to suffer frequently from toothaches. By some reports, Ludwig had just four teeth remaining at the time of his death. We can only imagine how painful it must have been for the king to have his teeth rot and fall out, one by one.

Prussian Crown Prince Friedrich met with Ludwig around this time and recorded his impressions of the king in his diary: "I find him strikingly changed. He has completely lost his good looks, and his front teeth are missing. He is pale, and he has a nervous, restless way of talking …"

The loss of his physical attractiveness was devastating to Ludwig, since he had always been so impressed by beauty, both in humans and in architecture. As his own looks deteriorated, he avoided being photographed whenever possible.

Even the king's gait changed. In an effort to imitate King Louis XIV's stride, he cultivated jerkier movements to replace his formerly graceful manner of walking and he swept his arms ahead of him, waving them across his path. One observer noted that the king's walk was "a total mockery of nature. Taking great strides he threw his long legs out in front of him as if he wanted to hurl them away from him, then he brought the front foot down as though with each step he was trying to crush a scorpion."

Perhaps in an attempt to avoid the people and paperwork that filled his days, Ludwig began doing most of his living at night. He got out of bed around 6 p.m. and spent time soaking in a bath sprinkled with perfume. Ludwig loved perfumes throughout his life, and had a large collection that he could choose from, depending on his mood. Sometimes, the king took cold baths in hopes of calming his restless mind. As his brother Otto descended into madness, cold baths were often prescribed for him as well.

After his bath, Ludwig typically spent time reading or studying his latest architectural project. "King Ludwig read … a great deal and on all manner of subjects," said his cabinet secretary's son-in-law. He also spent much time writing letters, both official and personal.

At midnight, it was time for the king's lunch, which he ate in solitude – who else would be available to join him at that hour, even if he had wanted company?

Then, it was time for Ludwig's favorite part of the day. He spent time outside (yes, in the dark), either walking in the fresh air or riding. The royal stables in Munich held around 500 horses, so he had his choice. A favorite activity involved Ludwig using a map to calculate the distance to a specific destination he wanted to visit (not an easy task in the days before the Internet). Ludwig then climbed onto a horse and rode that distance inside the Royal Riding Pavilion by circling the ring time after time, stopping to change horses when necessary. When his stopwatch told him he had ridden far enough to have arrived at his destination, the king hopped off his horse and shared a picnic lunch with the patient groom who had made this "journey" with him. Then, he "returned home" by riding the same distance, this time heading the opposite direction around the ring.

Around 1870, a horseback riding accident put an end to Ludwig's rides and contributed to his weight gain. From this time on, Ludwig rode behind his horses, either in a carriage or a sleigh.

Ludwig's sleigh was a sight to behold. It was all of gold, with carved cherubs. The cherubs lifted up a crown, which was powered with light to give off a soft glow. Four snow-white horses, their heads adorned with peacock feathers, pulled the sleigh across the snow. The riders were arrayed in a style that would have made Louis XIV proud: blue and silver dress coats, white knee breeches, long black riding boots, three-cornered hats, white gloves, and powdered white wigs. A messenger horse and rider, dressed in the same manner, rode ahead of the king's sleigh, and another valet rode standing on the back of the sleigh. Ludwig made quite an impression as he glided across the snowy Bavarian countryside.

Of course, most people never saw him, since these rides were made under cover of darkness. This was by design, since Ludwig hated being stared at. But as much as he disliked the government officials and courtiers of Munich, the king did love the common people of the countryside. Often during his night rides, he instructed the horses to stop and he got out to visit an undoubtedly surprised peasant family. Imagine your disbelief upon being awakened by a pounding at the door in the middle of the night. Opening the door slowly, you are greeted with an amazing sight: four beautiful white horses, their breath steaming in the cold air. Then you spy the grooms in their fine dress, and finally, you see your king stepping out of a golden sleigh! Is he really asking you humbly for a few hours to rest in your hut, or is this a dream?

This scene was replayed many times, and such events led the everyday Bavarian people to love Ludwig and refer to him as their "fairy king." He returned their affection, building numerous small huts in the mountains and heading to them as places of retreat and peace. This led to another of Ludwig's nicknames, "the Hermit of the Alps." The king enjoyed visiting various village festivals in the area. He got to know many of the country people personally, asking one how his crops were doing this year or another if his sick child had recovered. Always a cheerful giver, Ludwig left gifts for the folks he surprised with his night visits. Perhaps he saw these as a physical token to prove he had been there, in case the family wondered the next day whether his visit had been just a dream.

Ludwig often instructed his carriage or sleigh to stop in an Alpine meadow. Then, he might request that his grooms eat a picnic meal with him under a full moon. These picnics sometimes occurred during freezing winter nights. But Ludwig was undeterred by the cold, insisting to his companions that it was warm and sunny out. After eating, the king usually wanted to play blind man's bluff or another outdoor game with his servants. Were these unusual practices a way for Ludwig to try to reclaim the happy childhood he wished for? Or were they an example of budding insanity?

Perhaps surprisingly, music was not much of a passion for the king. He studied piano as a child, but after five years his teacher recommended that the lessons stop because Ludwig "has neither talent for music nor does he like it." What the king loved about Wagner's operas were the myths and tales themselves more than the music, although he did love the drama that filled

Wagner's music. Drama in all forms, from acting to costumes to scenery, touched Ludwig deeply.

No doubt, one of Ludwig's favorite pastimes was attending operas and other stage performances. He hated the audience staring at him while he watched, so he ordered command performances of various works for an audience of one: himself. These performances began in 1872 and continued for the next 13 years, when Ludwig's budget was slashed. They were numerous, consisting of 209 operas, dramas, and ballets. Ludwig frequently found inspiration from his reading, and when he read about an obscure play, he asked to see it performed.

Alone in his royal box at the theater, the king was free to cry, gasp, stand up, sit down, or react in any way he saw fit. "I go to look myself, not to provide a spectacle for others," he said. His passion was a boon for German artists and musicians, who were kept employed thanks to the king's patronage. One of the actors involved in these performances for the king declared them the most impressive and unforgettable of any during his forty years on stage.

Ludwig was often so emotionally moved by the stories enacted on stage that he requested that the actors visit him afterwards. Many of these actors made the mistake of feeling flattered that the king was interested in them personally, but Ludwig's fascination always revolved around the character rather than the actor himself.

Joseph Kainz was one such actor. Ludwig was so pleased with his portrayal of the character Didier in a play by Victor Hugo that he invited Kainz to Linderhof. However, when the actor appeared before the king, Ludwig was disappointed. Kainz seemed smaller in person, and his speaking manner was not the same as he had used to portray Didier.

A nearby servant took note of the king's displeasure and sneaked up to the actor, whispering, "Act, man, act!"

Kainz then began speaking to Ludwig, not in his normal voice, but as Didier.

This relieved the king, who invited "Didier" to the Moorish kiosk with him, where he listened to the actor reading aloud to him in his "heavenly voice" for several hours.

Although Ludwig mainly enjoyed the theater as an observer, he had a life-long love of dressing up in costume. He loved wearing the showiest of his royal robes, which emphasized his royal prestige. After his death, a swan costume was discovered among his things. No doubt he had worn it to impersonate his hero, the Swan Knight Lohengrin.

CHAPTER 12

Hall of Mirrors at Herrenchiemsee

HERRENCHIEMSEE

Ludwig now had a castle in the clouds and a jewel in the valley. For his next building project, he decided to replicate the French Palace of Versailles on an island.

Bavaria's largest lake, the Chiemsee (KEEM-say), was fifty miles southeast of Munich. It held two islands: Herreninsel ("men's island") and Fraueninsel ("women's island"). During medieval times, Herreninsel was home to a monastery. But the monks had long ago left the island, and now a timber company was seeking to buy it to cut down its dense forests. Ludwig didn't like this idea, so in 1873 he bought the island himself.

Unlike the valley setting of Linderhof, the island had ample space for a palace even bigger than Louis XIV's original Versailles masterpiece. Ludwig instructed his stage designers to create the palace as a tribute to royal magnificence. The result, Herrenchiemsee (Hair-un-KEEM-say), was indeed magnificent. Although only a small portion of the interior was ever completed, it still far surpassed the cost of any of Ludwig's other castles. He spent 6.2 million marks on Neuschwanstein, 8.5 million on Linderhof, and an astonishing 16.6 million on Herrenchiemsee. With even more castles in the works, we can only imagine how much the king would have ended up spending had he lived a normal lifespan.

Part of Herrenchiemsee's expenses resulted from its location. All materials had to be ferried across the Chiemsee to the island, and then transported to the island's center, where many of the magnificent trees Ludwig had bought the island to save had to be felled to make room for the huge palace.

Herrenchiemsee has a Neo Baroque style, with similarities to London's Buckingham Palace from the outside. Once inside, there's no question but that you've stepped into a special, and somewhat overwhelming, place.

The grand staircase rises from the midst of inlaid marble floors and marble walls, flanked by huge realistic murals, elaborate statues, and covered high above by a glass roof. Now you're up the stairs and ready to view the state apartments.

Put on your sunglasses before you enter the State Bedroom. It's incredibly dazzling, with almost every inch covered in some form of gold. Ludwig never intended to sleep in this room; it was a tribute to King Louis XIV. It's grander than anything even the Sun King created, with its stunning golden chandelier and enormous canopy bed. The bedding, embroidered in golden thread, took seven years for over twenty seamstresses to make. All the needlework in the room weighs three tons!

The Hall of Mirrors at Herrenchiemsee is a copy of the famous one at Versailles, but Ludwig's version is larger and more decorative than the original. The magnificent spectacle is 245 feet long (one-third longer than the original), 36 feet wide, and 42 feet high. Aiming for eternity and infinity, Ludwig ordered mirrors placed opposite each other down the hall's expanse to create depth. Alternating with the mirrors is a series of over forty candelabras and over thirty chandeliers, lit by 2000 candles. It was an amazing sight to see the candles flickering in the darkness, reflecting over and over in all the mirrors. Ludwig visited only at night, to appreciate the spectacle fully.

Ludwig's private bedroom looks less grand only when compared to the State Bedroom. Here, gold is interspersed with white and Ludwig's favorite color, blue. A large blue glass ball at the foot of the bed, mounted on an ornate golden base, fills the room with a peaceful blue glow when a candle inside is lit. The king was closely involved in the ball's production. He worked with a lighting expert for 18 months to ensure that the light produced was precisely the right shade of blue, with no white rays. Seamstresses spent years embroidering Ludwig's bedding.

But how many nights did Ludwig spend in this bed?

Only ten.

The king's only extended visit to his magnificent creation occurred at night during the autumn of 1885, when two boatmen in costumes rowed him to the island in a gondola.

Proceeding through the woods and into his palace, did Ludwig ever open doors onto the many unfinished portions of the building? Did he ever stare dejectedly at the huge brick and concrete room on the opposite side of the building from the grand staircase, housing just a construction site?

Once, he tapped his walking stick on a statue and was dismayed to find that it immediately shattered. With funds running short, the builders had substituted plaster for marble.

"Everything is false!" he cried, furious that his orders had been disobeyed.

Ludwig desired to surround himself with perfection. But in his castles, as in his life, his dreams often proved hollow. Their outer appeal masked an inner emptiness.

CHAPTER 13

Ludwig listens to Wagner play

TWILIGHT OF THE GODS

By 1870, the smothering friendship between Ludwig and Richard Wagner was basically over. While the king continued to savor every Wagner performance ("I need such joys if I am not to perish in the trivial whirlpool of everyday life," he wrote to the composer), the strong personalities of the two men had clashed too many times to allow a sunny relationship to continue.

To mark the third anniversary of their meeting, Ludwig had ordered a combination piano and writing desk for Wagner, so that he could more easily compose. But when Wagner arrived late to meet with the king, and in an unenthusiastic mood to boot, Ludwig decided to have the piece delivered to Hohenschwangau instead. It remains there to this day.

Another argument ensued when staging problems led to Wagner requesting a cancellation of his opera, *Das Rheingold*. Ludwig was furious at this move, writing to one of his court members, "The behavior of Wagner and the theatre rabble is absolutely criminal and impudent; it is an open revolt against My Orders, and this I will not allow! … The theatre people will obey My Orders and not Wagner's whims!"

Wagner's "Ring" operas caused more discord. *Der Ring des Nibelungen*, usually referred to as the Ring cycle, was a four-opera series. As the one paying the bills, Ludwig owned the rights to each of the four operas as they were completed. Wagner, however, wanted to wait for all four to be completed before any was performed individually. Ludwig went against these wishes and staged the first two operas before the final two were finished. This led Wagner to lie to Ludwig about when he actually completed the third opera.

Yet another crack in the friendship involved Ludwig ordering Wagner to replace certain singers in a *Lohengrin* production, because he disliked them. Wagner was angry at this and stormed back to Switzerland.

And yet, both men's personalities were prone to bouts of intense anger followed by another round of admiration. Ludwig wrote to Wagner's wife, "Oh, he [Wagner] is godlike, godlike! My mission is to live for Him, to suffer for Him."

Wagner likewise was often full of praise for his benefactor. "What he has done for me will far outlast my span of life."

Despite their disappointment over the lack of support for a Munich Opera House, Ludwig and the composer had never given up the dream of a venue suitable for Wagner's sagas.

During the spring of 1872, Wagner was considering the northern Bavarian city of Bayreuth as a possible location. After the hostile reception he had received in Munich, he had no interest in exploring options there. For the time being, the composer kept Ludwig in the dark about his plans.

Bayreuth was home of the Margrave's Opera House, which boasted the largest opera stage in Germany. However, a visit there convinced Wagner that even this space was too small for the major operas he was composing. Additionally, the grand décor inside was unsuitable for his Ring operas, which required a more austere setting so that the music could command center stage. Seeing no way to renovate the building, Wagner insisted on starting his Festspielhaus (festival theater) from scratch.

The fundraising began, with the city of Bayreuth donating the land and Ludwig giving Wagner money to build a house. The composer traveled throughout Europe, giving lectures and concerts to earn more money. When all this resulted in insufficient funds, Wagner resorted to his usual tactic: he asked the king for funding. But this time, Ludwig refused. He now needed all the money available to him for his own building projects.

Wagner brainstormed a list of any possible contributors to his opera house, appealing to Prussia and various European leaders. Finally, Ludwig gave in to the repeated requests and provided more money, on the condition that it was a loan only and must eventually be repaid. After both men died, payments were still being made.

The Festspielhaus was completed in 1876, four years after it was begun. To this day, members of the Wagner family own it, and only works by Richard Wagner are performed there. The inside of the theater was more spartan than the traditionally lavish theaters of the late nineteenth century. The seats and much of the interior were made of wood, which created a better acoustic environment for the singers and musicians. Wager designed the orchestra pit to be recessed beneath the stage and hidden by a hood, so that the audience would focus their attention on the acting and singing onstage.

In August of 1876, the hall was ready for its first performance of the complete four-opera Ring cycle. Wishing to avoid the crowds, Ludwig decided to attend the dress rehearsals instead of the actual performances. He and Wagner met for the first time in eight years. Time had not been kind to either. Wagner appeared frail, older, and more hunched than he had been previously, and Ludwig had become heavy and awkward in his movements, sporting a beard as well.

But the passing of years had not dampened the king's enthusiasm for Wagner's staging of his favorite German tales. Four consecutive nights of watching the opera performances moved him beyond words, and the few other spectators in the theater saw him shaking, crying, and gripping the arms of his chair as the music swelled. He wrote to Wagner, "I came with great expectations; and, high though these were, they were far, far exceeded."

So touched was he that he braved the crowds to attend all four performances again later in the month. At the conclusion of the final opera, Wagner praised Ludwig from the stage as "co-creator" of the cycle, a tribute the king accepted gratefully. Many of Wagner's world-famous operas would never have been produced if not for Ludwig, the generous benefactor who avoided crowds at all cost.

Pleased with the Ring performances, Wagner settled in at his Bayreuth home, called Wahnfried (VAHN-freed) ("peace from life's madness"). There he began work on his final opera, *Parsifal*. This was based on – you guessed it – another German legend.

Wagner's composing and Ludwig's building projects kept the two apart, but they met again in 1881 for a performance of *Lohengrin* – significant, since this was the opera that had first attracted the king to the composer's work. Ludwig invited the Great Friend to dine with him in his beloved winter garden. But both men's egos had grown over the years, and they clashed days later when Wagner planned to conduct the prelude to *Parsifal* for the king. Ludwig arrived late, which annoyed Wagner. The king further frustrated the composer by requesting that he conduct the prelude a second time. Not sensing Wagner's growing anger, Ludwig continued with a request for the prelude from *Lohengrin* so that he could compare the two. Wagner angrily stormed from the room, leaving his conducting baton with an assistant.

While they resumed a friendly correspondence by mail, the two never met again.

Wagner moved to Italy in an attempt to improve his failing health, and on February 13, 1883, he suffered a heart attack. The youngest of nine children born to a poor family, now one of the most famous opera composers of all time, he died at his desk, working to the end.

In Munich, servants informed Ludwig. His face grew stony, and he shouted, "He is dead?" and proceeded to stomp the floor so powerfully that a floor tile broke. From this day forward, the king ordered that all pianos in his castles be shrouded in black crepe. The melodies of the Great Friend's music never again sounded in the halls of his residences, as this was too painful for Ludwig to bear.

A train carried the composer's body from Venice back to Bayreuth for burial. When the train passed through Munich, hundreds of mourners draped the train station in black and stood by to pay their respects. The king had a valet deliver a large wreath of laurels, bearing the inscription "To the Composer of Words and Music, the Maestro Richard Wagner, from Ludwig II of Bavaria." His grief and desire for isolation kept him from attending the funeral.

The Great Friend was buried in the garden at Wahnfried, next to his beloved dog, Russ. At the entrance to the house stands a bust of Ludwig, who made much of Wagner's success possible. "If I had not found him [Ludwig] everything was at an end for me – everything," Wagner once wrote. In Ludwig, Wagner had found what he needed: a powerful advocate with the means to finance his ambitions. Unfortunately, Ludwig never found such a benefactor for his own dreams.

Ludwig felt that his patronage of Wagner was one of the greatest ways he could serve his people. And indeed, Wagner's music is still famous throughout the world, particularly in Germany. Almost everyone recognizes "Here

Comes the Bride" – its melody comes from *Lohengrin*. By providing inspiring music to Bavarians, Ludwig hoped that they would gain an appreciation for beauty. "When we two have long been dead, our work will still be a shining example to distant posterity, a delight to the centuries," the king had written to Wagner years ago, when the friends had first met. "And hearts will glow with enthusiasm for art, the God-given, the eternally living."

CHAPTER 14

Ludwig and Otto as children

FAIRY TALE KING, ECCENTRIC, OR INSANE?

Bavaria is just a state in southern Germany. It's not even a country, and it doesn't have a king anymore. So why are we still fascinated by a man who ruled it over one hundred years ago? Why aren't we as interested in Ludwig's grandfather, King Ludwig I? Or perhaps Leopold I, who ruled Belgium during that time, or William III, King of the Netherlands?

Perhaps it's because mystery continues to surround Ludwig. During his lifetime, and even today, we're not sure: was he a fairy tale king? Eccentric? Or insane?

Many of the rural Bavarian commoners considered Ludwig their Märchen-könig, or Fairy Tale King. No wonder; fairy tales feature fantastic forces and characters, and Ludwig was certainly fantastic. He stopped in to see many of his people during night rides, accompanied by undoubtedly fairy-tale-looking wigged footmen and dreamy white horses.

Ludwig the Fairy Tale King was kind to others. He had never really liked his childhood teacher, La Rosee, yet when the king learned that La Rosee was dying, Ludwig promoted him to the rank of Major General and provided him a personal suite where he lived the rest of his life in security. Ludwig loved to give gifts and flowers, and he showered them on his mother and Sisi, as well as strangers. Always, he gave without fanfare and without alerting the press.

Although he shunned much of humanity, there were exceptions. Just a few years before his death, Ludwig took a special interest in his cousin, Prince Ludwig Ferdinand. Ludwig Ferdinand married a Spanish princess whom King Ludwig found charming. He invited the couple to a cozy dinner in his winter garden, and spent much time with them. At the princess's request, he offered her a rare tour of Herrenchiemsee. She thought the king was delightful, writing, "This man has something great and poetic about him, and has powers of imagination such as one rarely finds in anyone."

Ludwig loved fairy tale mountain settings, which were plentiful in Bavaria. He spent much of his time nestled in his various mountain retreats, far from prying eyes and only accessible to animals, which he loved. As a king, his favorites are no surprise: horses, peacocks, swans, and falcons. The only animal he disliked was the vulture, because its brutal nature disturbed his sensitive spirit.

From his high mountain bungalows, Ludwig could indulge in his splendid thoughts. Isolated from the world, he could almost convince himself that he was Lohengrin, the swan knight. Just as Lohengrin was misunderstood, so Ludwig felt unfairly judged by his officials.

Most of Ludwig's excesses involved pursuits popular among Bavarians, who shared his love for hiking, drinking, and over-the-top decorating. These passions endeared him to his people. They accepted this stubborn, quiet, handsome king as their own Prince Charming.

Yet for all his fairy tale charm, some – notably, much of the royal court and residents of Munich – described Ludwig as eccentric rather than as a fairy tale king.

Eccentric: deviating from conventional conduct, especially in odd or whimsical ways.

Some of Ludwig's behaviors definitely exceeded a "fairy tale" description and veered into eccentricity. No doubt part of this was due to the king's genetic heritage. More of it sprang from his isolation. Ludwig was a true introvert, preferring to be alone rather than in company.

The king went to great lengths to avoid contact with others. He disliked ambassadors and other government representatives, and met with them as rarely as possible, frequently feigning illness as an excuse to cancel scheduled meetings. When he absolutely had to attend an official dinner, he arranged to sit behind a large plant or other table decoration, and he instructed the musicians to play as loudly as possible in order to reduce the amount of polite conversation he would be expected to make. Ludwig steeled himself for the torture of these dinners by drinking up to ten glasses of champagne before they began.

But Ludwig's desire to be alone only increased many of his odd behaviors. Time spent in his inner world of thoughts and dreams made it more difficult to return to reality, and Ludwig "visited" the real world less and less frequently. This is not to say that the king was happy with his solitary state. "You understand me so well, and only a very few people do," he wrote to Baroness Leonrod. "By most of them I am misunderstood so that, naturally, I felt rebuked by the world and retire more and more."

Perhaps loneliness led him to visit his cousin Ludwig Ferdinand's home unannounced one evening, only to spend a long period gazing longingly at Ludwig Ferdinand's 10-month-old baby, sleeping in his crib. Ludwig later wrote to his cousin, explaining that he had never before seen a baby close-up.

One of Ludwig's valets told the king how much his people loved him, and encouraged him to appear before them in Munich. "I cannot," the king replied. "It is frightful, but I can no longer bear to be stared at by thousands of people, to smile and to extend greetings a thousand times, to ask questions of people who mean nothing to me and to listen to answers that do not interest me. No, no! There is no longer any escape from my solitude. Sometimes, when I have read myself to exhaustion and everything is quiet, I have an irresistible urge to hear a human voice. Then I call one of the domestic servants … and ask him to tell me about his home and his family. Otherwise I would completely forget the art of speech."

Other than his cousin Sisi, Ludwig had no close friends. This lack of allies helped lead to his downfall. Most of the quirky behaviors attributed to Ludwig were reported by those serving him. And all those hours spent alone provided him with plenty of time to develop behaviors that could only be described as odd.

His unusual behaviors included dining alone … and yet, not alone. Ludwig always requested that his dinners be prepared for three or four guests. The king then dined with whomever he pleased, pretending to have dinner discussions with King Louis XIV, or Marie Antoinette, or their friends. Ludwig's self-setting tables ensured that servants could not listen in on these conversations.

Once, the king requested that his favorite horse, Cosa Rara, eat a multicourse dinner with him in his dining room. The horse was understandably confused, and proceeded to smash the dishes and table.

Ludwig's behavior included various rituals. In honor of Marie Antoinette, whose history Ludwig could never read "without being deeply moved," the king erected a bust at Linderhof depicting the French queen. Each time he passed it, Ludwig removed his hat, bowed, and stroked its cheeks. He stopped and kissed a special column at Linderhof as well each time he passed it.

As a boss, Ludwig was no fairy tale king. His servants reported that he forbade them from looking at him. Many of Ludwig's odd requests (requiring servants to bow low and back out of rooms, for instance) were actually his effort to copy habits of the Bourbon French court, but in his times, they were seen as another example of eccentricity.

Ludwig commanded that various servants who offended him in even minor ways be flogged, skinned alive, or executed. Happily, these sentences were not actually carried out, nor did the king seem upset if he noticed that none of the wayward servants disappeared.

In a note, the king described the punishment he ordered for one servant: "Have his head roughly banged against the wall. For three days, whenever he comes into My Presence he must kneel with his head on the floor … and must remain kneeling until I give him permission to rise; this must be firmly drilled into him. For three hours of each of the three days when he is shut up, you must yourself tie his hands in order to bring him into submission, humbly, otherwise it is all up with him and his life will be made a misery for him."

Ludwig placed strict, peculiar demands on his servants, and he became furious if they deviated from these even slightly. "Every time I have to retie my tie, so badly, so impossibly has the fellow done it," he wrote to one servant, complaining about another. "It is scandal; the assurance that it will be done better next time is completely valueless if it is not fulfilled. Speak to him about it and show him how to do it better." Details mattered to the king: "Thierry must be told exactly how I want the new tea set so that there shall be no confusion. It is not to be Chinese and not Japanese. The blue must be purer and more radiating as on the vase."

Since he disliked speaking to his servants, the king often communicated with them via notes. These would prove hurtful to Ludwig as many of them were later used as evidence of his insanity. Whether they show a ruler who is insane or merely quirky and controlling, they do offer a glimpse into how difficult it must have been to work for him. "Osterholzer shall be told that he has not to grow a moustache; shall not shorten it either … I expect it so. It never has to be that when my room is got ready for the night the window is left open. Horrible nonsense."

Ludwig could be physically rough with his servants, sometimes kicking and hitting them. He scared cabinet secretary Friedrich Ziegler half to death once, when Ziegler was reading a report to the king. Ludwig removed a small gun from his desk and pointed it directly at Ziegler, who stopped reading for fear of what was coming next. But the king twirled the gun in the air as a signal for the cabinet secretary to keep reading. Ziegler continued, only to see Ludwig again aim the gun at him. This back-and-forth went on for several minutes, apparently amusing the king. Ziegler was understandably shaken, because this incident went beyond the usual even for Ludwig. Ziegler resigned in 1879, returned at the king's request in 1880, but in 1883 he left for good, suffering from nervous exhaustion and unable to continue working in such a stressful environment. The king did recognize the demands he placed on his employees, once saying, "I wouldn't be my own cabinet secretary for anything in the world."

Insane: mentally disordered; in a state of mind that prevents normal perception, behavior, or social interaction; seriously mentally ill.

Now we must consider whether Ludwig's behaviors went beyond a fairy tale or eccentric definition, and into full-blown insanity. He's known today as "Mad King Ludwig." Is this title deserved?

Ludwig grew up knowing about the mental problems many of his relatives faced. He had been concerned about his father's insane sister, his Aunt Alexandra, since childhood. And insanity was always close to him in the person of his younger brother, Otto. In his twenties, Otto's mental health had declined to the point where Ludwig ordered him confined to Nymphenburg Palace, where the two boys had been born. His brother's condition was quite troubling to Ludwig, who wrote, "Otto's state is deplorable. He is in the best way of becoming just like Aunt Alexandra; he suffers from a morbid over-excitement of the whole nervous system which is quite terrible."

Otto seldom dressed during the day, "often looks like a wild animal," and disliked going outside, complaining that his feet were covered in boils (although these boils weren't visible to anyone else). He kept his boots on, sometimes for weeks at a time, and spent his days making faces and barking like a dog. Ludwig often discovered his brother sitting alone in a darkened room, refusing to leave. Otto rarely spoke to Ludwig, but insisted that he heard voices in his head calling out to him and shouting at him.

Despite his mental state, Otto was unhappy with his confinement at Nymphenburg. "You have no right, seeing that I have done no wrong, to treat me thus," he wrote to Ludwig. "I have submitted to duress and I am a prisoner; my treatment has been disgraceful." But the king, advised by mental instability expert Doctor Bernhard von Gudden, kept his brother confined. Considering Doctor von Gudden's later appearance in our tale, perhaps Ludwig should have sought a second opinion.

By age thirty, Otto needed more than he could get from mere servants at Nymphenburg. He was officially declared insane, and was moved to Schloss Fürstenried, a castle on the far outskirts of Munich. Otto's condition was so disturbing that his mother, who had always preferred Otto over Ludwig, rarely visited her younger son here because his behavior was too upsetting to her.

In that time period, "moral treatment" was the prevailing method of care for the mentally ill. This involved treating patients like children, and insisting that they live in a structured, regulated environment. Patients were expected to eat at the table, show good manners, and make polite conversation. They were constantly monitored to ensure that they were complying with guidelines, and the hope was that such a normal way of living would restore patients' mental health.

Whether he was rebelling against these rules or simply couldn't help himself, Otto was not a cooperative patient. He let out blood-curdling screams at all hours of the day and night. His walls had to be padded because he banged his head against them. He refused to eat as a prince – or even a normal person – would, tearing his food apart with his hands. He smashed flies against windows, and during quieter moments, played with toys Ludwig sent to him.

The king was terrified by Otto's illness. Ludwig had a history of hearing footsteps and voices that others were unaware of, and each time this happened, he was struck with panic that he would end up like his brother. In the royal court, many of the king's servants and officials whispered about Ludwig's quirks and discussed whether they indicated his own descent into insanity.

The king's odd behaviors never descended to the level of Otto, but they were disturbing nonetheless. He told horrified servants of a dream where he dug up his father from his coffin and boxed his ears, and another where he broke a large jug of water over his mother's head, dragged her about on the ground, and stomped her with his heels.

Speaking to an author the year he died, Ludwig conveyed his angst over all the discussion of his supposed insanity: "Insults wound me so deeply that they disarm me, they force me to the ground, and I am sure that they will one day destroy me .... A great part of what is taken for madness is really hyper-sensitiveness. It has often been maliciously hinted and even openly declared that I am a fool. Maybe I am, but I doubt it ... .A real madman is as a rule the only person who doesn't recognize his madness .... If I were a poet, I might be able to reap praise by putting these things to verse. But the talent of expression was not given to me, and so I must bear being laughed at, scorned at, and slandered. I am called a fool. Will God call me a fool when I am summoned before him?"

Some evidences given of Ludwig's apparent madness seem humorous to us today: one counselor offered as proof of insanity Ludwig's commission of an inventor to create an aircraft that would allow the king to fly over the Bavarian Alps. Less than twenty years after his death, Ludwig's "crazy" idea became a reality.

Fairy Tale king, eccentric ruler, or Mad King Ludwig? You decide. Cousin Sisi was probably close to the truth when she declared, "He is not mad enough to be locked up, but too abnormal to manage comfortably in the world with reasonable people." While it was Ludwig's fortune to be king – and therefore possess the means to build his magnificent castles – his royal status was also his misfortune, since it focused on him many eyes determined to see his downfall.

A fairy tale is defined as a story featuring fantastic forces and characters, where improbable events lead to a happy ending. Ludwig's tale involved fantastic forces and characters to be sure, and improbable events as well. The happy ending, unfortunately, is missing.

CHAPTER 15

Neuschwanstein during construction

THE MONEY RUNS OUT

"I must build or die," Ludwig once said. By the 1880s, this had become a problem, because even though he was king, not even Ludwig had unlimited funding. Many people think that the king bankrupted Bavaria by building his castles, but this isn't true. Ludwig built using his own money and the money from his civil list (a civil list is an amount of money paid to various members of the royal family each year as a salary). The king's civil list amounted to around two million marks each year, and by 1884 he had borrowed against future civil list payments to the extent that he was over eight millions marks in debt.

Ludwig hoped to build even more castles beyond his current three creations. He had plans for three more. He dreamed of a Byzantine palace similar to his Moorish kiosk at Linderhof, and a Chinese palace where Ludwig and his servants could live like members of the Chinese imperial court. He also envisioned another gothic castle, to be called Falkenstein after the name of the medieval ruins currently on the mountaintop. Ludwig purchased the Falkenstein site in 1883 and commissioned Christian Jank (Neuschwanstein's designer) to draw up plans. Aware of the king's debts, Jank created a modest design for the castle. Furious, Ludwig replaced him with another designer, who satisfied the king with plans for a gothic edifice with even more spires and towers than Neuschwanstein. By 1884, a road had already been constructed up the mountain to the building site.

But work on these new castles was put on hold indefinitely. Workers at Herrenchiemsee and Neuschwanstein had threatened to stop if they were not paid. Ludwig panicked. He had eliminated many typical royal expenses – notably, state dinners and balls – in order to continue his one true passion, building. But now, even this economizing was not enough. He needed to come up with more money! How could he do it?

Ludwig suffered greatly over his lack of funding, and his toothaches and headaches made more frequent appearances. His desperation increased when he realized that the government might seize his castles if he could not come up with a way to pay his debts. The king's relationship with his own government officials had never been warm, but by now it was positively icy.

In 1880, Johann von Lutz became prime minister. Lutz had worked in government jobs for years, going way back to the days when he was sent to give Richard Wagner Ludwig's note banishing the composer from Bavaria. Ambitious and power-hungry, Lutz observed that Ludwig was uninterested in government, and seized upon this opportunity to grab power for himself. Over the years, he cut off the king more and more from decision-making, and took over many of the king's responsibilities. Lutz was only too happy to rule in Ludwig's absence, but his actions isolated Ludwig even further from those who might have helped him brainstorm ways out of his financial crisis.

What could the king do to get his hands on more money? Perhaps he could approach friends, but Ludwig had very few. Frantic, he dropped his pride and sent servants to other kings and rulers to ask for funds. Mainly, he sent out emissaries across Europe, but he ordered others as far as Persia and Turkey to request money for his architectural creations. Understandably, many of those sent out to beg for money were less than enthusiastic about their mission. But Ludwig threatened to fire anyone who refused to carry out his wishes, and so they went, heads bowed and requests in hand.

Ludwig was dismayed when his efforts were largely unsuccessful. German Emperor Wilhelm, annoyed by Ludwig's financial excesses, gave the king no money outright. He did, however, offer his nephew a loan with the stipulation that it must be used to reduce debt and not to finance more building. Angered, Ludwig turned this down.

By 1885, the situation was worse. Ludwig was now fourteen million marks in debt. His cabinet recommended extreme economizing and a complete halt to all building projects. "That I have not been happy for months has to do with the buildings," he wrote to his mother. He visited her at Hohenschwangau in October for her sixtieth birthday, and rejected her offer to give him all of her personal wealth, including her jewels, to apply to his castles. The two never saw each other again.

Distraught and seeing no way out of his financial hole, Ludwig decided against his usual autumn stay in Munich. The Bavarian constitution required the monarch to spend twenty-one nights each year in the capital, and Ludwig rarely exceeded this bare minimum. He remained in the comfort of his isolated castles, far from the critical eyes of Munich's people and officials. But this turned out to be another poor decision by the king. Imagine that a U.S. President decided to stop spending time in Washington, D. C. The press would criticize him for this, and that's exactly what happened to Ludwig. The newspapers weren't the only ones speaking ill of the king.

One newspaper reported, "Nowadays it seems as if any scoundrel thinks he has the right to criticize and insult His Majesty. It almost looks like an organized system of calumniation; as though the idea is to alienate at any price and eventually get rid of the King." Its foreboding later proved true. The criticism of Ludwig by the media and by the officials and citizens became a vicious cycle, cementing public opinion against the king. Feeling more and more victimized, Ludwig decided to conduct all government business by correspondence rather than face-to-face. His cabinet was outraged that the king could find time to design castles and attend gatherings with his own servants, yet refused to meet with them. Ludwig was nudged even further out of the loop within his own government.

The year 1886 saw no improvement to the financial mess, and Ludwig threatened to kill himself if the planned confiscations of Linderhof and Herrenchiemsee occurred. Feeling that his options were disappearing, the king sent out servants again. But this time, instead of sending them to request funds from rulers, he ordered them to rob all the banks in London, Paris, Berlin, and Frankfurt. Of course they didn't follow through on this, but they did their best to convince the king they had at least tried. One aide told another that he couldn't give a message to the king, because "I'm in Naples at the moment."

"Whatever can you mean?" the aide questioned.

"The king sent me to Naples; but there was no point in going, so I stayed here. But I said I was going and that I would not be back until Wednesday, so I cannot announce my return before that." Doubtless, it was especially exhausting to work for Ludwig during this time.

Adding to Ludwig's troubles was the stipulation in Bavaria that creditors could sue the ruling king. This actually happened in April 1886, when the company supplying his castles with water and gas sued Ludwig for non-payment. This was a huge embarrassment for the cabinet, and Prime Minister Lutz decided it was time to take action against the king.

The cabinet informed Ludwig that he must stop his expensive building and return to the "economical methods" his father had used. He was to avoid further building projects, and curtail his "strange and costly visits to the Alpine castles." They further requested that Ludwig return at once to Munich, dismiss his personal staff, and meet in person with the cabinet. Too late, Ludwig realized that his isolation had eroded the royal sovereignty he valued so highly. He threatened to dismiss the entire cabinet.

Munich was in an uproar over the deteriorating relationship between the king and cabinet. Several high-ranking Munich businessmen wrote Ludwig a letter, begging him to return to the capital regularly if not permanently, and also offering to pay the king's debts. But a Lutz–approved "unofficial censor" intercepted the letter, and it never reached the king.

Members of Ludwig's Wittelsbach family watched this drama with worry. They had ruled Bavaria for over 700 years, since 1180. Yet many of them feared that Ludwig's spending would use up the family fortune in a single generation.

Johann Lutz took note of all this and must have laughed gleefully. Ludwig was playing right into his hands, providing all the evidence Lutz needed to plot a total overthrow of the king. Lutz was anxious to put an end to Ludwig's extravagance and nonsense. All he needed was proof that the king was insane, and Lutz already had it.

CHAPTER 16

Johann Lutz

THE BIG BAD WOLF

Every fairy tale needs a villain, whether it's a witch, an evil stepmother, or perhaps a big bad wolf. Johann Lutz plays the role of the big bad wolf in our story.

During the summer of 1885, Ludwig's uncle, Prince Luitpold, called Lutz for a meeting. Luitpold was sixty-four, a shy and retiring man who was a brother to Ludwig's father, the late King Maximilian II. Luitpold and his nephew Ludwig were not close, but Luitpold held a high position within the royal family. Ludwig's brother Otto was second in line to the throne, and Luitpold was third. Since Otto was obviously in no condition to rule, Luitpold realized that he was really next to Ludwig in the practical order of succession.

His nearness to the throne made Luitpold extra sensitive toward all the controversy over Ludwig's financial mismanagement. Luitpold saw himself as the head of the Wittelsbachs, and he feared that his nephew was damaging the family, both socially and financially. He visited Prime Minister Lutz in hopes of coming up with a solution that could restore the family's good name. However, Lutz wasn't as concerned about the Wittelsbach family's reputation as he was with getting rid of Ludwig and retaining his own power. He was thrilled when Luitpold requested a meeting. This meant that he had the royal family's tacit approval for taking action against the king!

During their meeting, the two men came up with three areas where Ludwig was vulnerable. The first was his finances. While it was true that the king had used his own funds for his building projects, he had crossed the line when he ordered employees to secure loans for him, threatening them with dismissal if they failed. This brought his financial troubles into the realm of government function, and it was unacceptable.

Ludwig's second weakness involved his disdain for his public duties. Over the years, the king had retreated further and further into solitude. He conducted almost all of his business by correspondence, rarely meeting with anyone involved with the government. He spent very little time in the capital, which was disturbing to his people and his government officials alike. Ludwig's grandfather, Ludwig I, had cautioned, "A function that remains unexercised is soon lost altogether." In failing to "exercise" his royal duties, the king had lost much of the skill necessary to carry them out at all.

Lutz and Luitpold agreed that Ludwig was an ineffective leader in both these areas, and yet felt that neither reason was strong enough to merit his removal as king. After all, Ludwig might stop his building projects, eliminating much of the financial problems. Although it was unlikely, it was possible that he might also do a turn-around and begin meeting again with his officials and spending time in Munich. No, another area of vulnerability must be found – one that Ludwig could not overcome.

The men's eyes met. This was "Mad King Ludwig" they were dealing with! That was it: insanity. The Bavarian constitution stated that a regency could be established if a king were mentally unstable. A regency meant that someone else could rule in the king's place. Since he was the closest mentally-stable person to the throne, Prince Luitpold was the obvious choice for regent. It's probably no surprise that Lutz eagerly offered to stay on in his position as prime minister. Lutz knew that Luitpold had little desire for power, and so the prime minister planned to basically rule Bavaria from that role.

But was Ludwig truly insane? This was of little importance, because the constitution just mentioned an *appearance* of insanity. Lutz already had several of Ludwig's servants spying on the king and reporting evidence of the king's "insanity" back to him. Lutz was also well aware that the king had few friends left among the citizens and politicians in Munich to contradict any excoriating evidence.

However, Ludwig did have plenty of admirers among the rural Bavarians. And Luitpold had no burning desire to rule as king. His personality was not suited to it, and his main goal was simply to stop the damage to the Wittelsbach name and fortune. Lutz knew that he would need to proceed slowly and cautiously to avoid an uprising of Ludwig's supporters, and Luitpold reluctantly agreed to help. The last thing either man wanted was a Bavarian civil war.

Lutz formed a commission to support his scheme. He dispatched a messenger to Bismarck, Chancellor of the German Empire, trying to get a feel for whether he would object to a plot to remove Ludwig. Bismarck sent word that Prussia would not interfere in what he considered Bavarian business.

The next hurdle was to get a doctor's report indicating that Ludwig was insane. The servants' stories were colorful and alarming, but an actual physician's report would look more official, Lutz thought. For this duty, he selected Dr. Bernhard von Gudden, director of the General Lunatic Asylum of Upper Bavaria. You'll remember that Dr. Gudden had been one of the doctors working with the king's brother, Otto. The sixty-one-year-old physician was considered an expert on insanity. He met with Lutz on March 23, 1886, to discuss writing up a formal paper detailing the king's mental condition. Among its pronouncements, Gudden offered this hopeless appraisal: "Your Majesty is in a very advanced stage of mental disorder, a form of insanity known to brain specialists by the name of 'Paranoia.' As this form of brain-trouble has a slow but progressive development of many years duration, Your Majesty must be regarded as incurable, a still further decline of the mental powers being the natural development of the disease. Suffering from such a disorder, freedom of action can no longer be allowed and Your Majesty is declared to be incapable of ruling, which incapacity will be not only for a year's duration but for the length of Your Majesty's life."

There was a major problem with this report. None of the four doctors signing on to it, including Dr. Gudden, had ever examined Ludwig. It was written based totally on hearsay and testimony from servants. Many of these servants told their increasingly bizarre tales only after financial rewards were offered to those testifying in support of the king's insanity. They told of a ruler whose behavior could indicate insanity: "His majesty loses control of his limbs at times, being capable in anger of dancing a demoniacal dislocated kind of dance, ghastly to see, beating the air with his arms like a wild man." Others told tales of a king who insisted on eating outdoors when the temperature was below zero, but also taking walks with an overcoat and umbrella on hot summer days.

Should servants make a mistake, they reported that the king required them to demonstrate their apology by lying flat on the floor. They were never to look at the king, and one servant claimed that Ludwig had required him to wear a black mask for a year after he had accidentally made eye contact with the monarch.

It must have taken courage to stand up for Ludwig in the hostile environment created by the Lutz regime, but a few brave souls did just that. Two aides refused to cooperate with the commission, arguing that the king was perfectly sane. They were never called to testify on his behalf. Ludwig's cabinet secretary contacted Lutz, telling him that he had over 300 notes and letters from the king that showed no evidence of insanity. Servants spoke out: "I could observe no signs of the alleged mental illness of the king. Nor could I perceive any abnormal changes. I always stayed close to the king. I dressed him and served him. He often talked to me. Never did the king show any sign of mental illness."

From another: "In the last days of his life, I was often assigned to the king's personal service, and I can only say that he was a good and just master. Although he sometimes scolded and stormed, when someone had done something wrong, his anger usually blew over quickly. I myself never heard about or saw any crazy orders being given, such as scratching at doors for admittance, lying down and having to crawl on the floor, wearing masks and so on. My fellow servant Mayr, who later told so many bad things of the king, often talked to me about the king. If the things he declared had really happened, he would surely have told me about them sooner. On the contrary! I was often surprised of how calm and composed the king was in the last days of his life, when he had to recognize the vastness of the betrayal."

But Lutz ignored any information that could have vindicated the king. He had been happy to encourage Ludwig's isolation, and now he was happy to hear of quirks the solitary king had developed. He disregarded any evidence that didn't support his contention that Ludwig was insane.

Ludwig was apparently unaware that the government was plotting his downfall, although he knew that he was not popular with officials. "It seems to me that in the household of life, there is only room for a single type of person," he said. "Whoever is different, is called eccentric by friend and foe." He was still feeling the enormous stress created by his growing debt, but the king was in a relatively content state in June 1886. May, always his favorite month, (he dubbed it "the month of rapture") had just ended, and he was spending some relaxing days at Neuschwanstein. He was oblivious to the intrigue Lutz was plotting from Munich.

On June 7, the doctors who had reviewed evidence from Ludwig's servants met. They agreed that they needed no personal observation of the king to draw up their report, and wrote in conclusion:

The mental powers of His Majesty are disrupted to such an extent that all judgment is lacking, and his thinking is in total contradiction with reality ... Gripped by the illusion that he holds absolute power in abundance and made lonely by self-isolation, he stands like a blind man without a guide at the edge of a precipice.

Joining Ludwig at the precipice were the doctors, Lutz, Luitpold, and the other government officials. How would this fairy tale end?

CHAPTER 17

Tower at Neuschwanstein

NOT SO HAPPILY EVER AFTER

June 2, 1886, in America: President Grover Cleveland married Frances Folsom in the White House, becoming the only president to wed there. Just weeks earlier, pharmacist John Pemberton invented Coca Cola in a brass kettle in his backyard.

June 7, 1886, in Munich, events were quite different. The sun shone, pleasantly warm on the city streets. Horses' hooves clopped as they pulled carriages along the streets, and life went on as usual. But drama was unfolding in a meeting of the Bavarian cabinet. With the doctors' report in hand, the ministers agreed that Ludwig could not continue to reign, given the seriousness of his mental condition. Lutz appointed a seven-member commission to arrest the king and give him a letter from Luitpold, informing him of his deposition. Should Ludwig somehow manage to remain king, all the cabinet ministers planned to resign. Lutz and Prince Luitpold ordered that the constitutional process to establish a regency begin immediately. They gave the army special orders to enforce loyalty to the new leaders, and warned them to be on the lookout for any popular uprisings in Ludwig's defense. As soon as the commission could send word that Ludwig was under arrest, Prince Luitpold's regency was to be announced to the citizens. A session of parliament was called for June 15 to deal with any problems that might arise.

And so, the ending to Ludwig's reign was planned. The next day, June 8, the delegation of seven left Munich to set their plans into motion.

Meanwhile, at Neuschwanstein, Ludwig awoke at 2:00 p.m., which was early by his standards. Telling servants he felt restless, he paced the vast, unfinished rooms of his castle, peering out at the mountains and surveying the golden splendor of his throne room. How magnificent it would look once the throne arrived! Yet not even the throne room's splendor calmed him on this day; something was troubling him. Perhaps it was the heavy mist in the air. From the throne room balcony, Ludwig noted the tiny water droplets clinging to each fir branch. He ate his traditional midnight lunch, and prepared for a 1:00 a.m. carriage ride.

About the time Ludwig woke, the delegation to arrest him was arriving at Hohenschwangau. Despite the care they took with their report to depose the king, they had mistaken the castle he was staying at. Discovering their error, they decided to stay at Hohenschwangau and indulge in a seven-course meal before journeying to Neuschwanstein. Drinking forty quarts of beer and ten bottles of champagne, the men began to argue over their next steps. Should they bring a straitjacket along? After all, the king was a man of great size and strength. Some argued that the restraint was necessary; others disliked the idea, feeling that its use would be demeaning to the king.

Where should they take the king? Originally, the commissioners considered Fürstenried, where Prince Otto was confined. They also considered

Linderhof. But the men realized that the many peasants and villagers living near the palace were quite fond of Ludwig. They loved their fairy tale king and benefited from his wealth, since he employed many of them when he was in residence. The king's largesse played a major role in Bavarians' lives, whether it paid for clearing paths for his midnight rides or planting overnight flower meadows. With Linderhof rejected as a prison, the commission decided to drive the king to Berg Castle, which was easier to secure. On the shores of Lake Starnberg, Berg Castle was also close to Munich. This would make it more convenient for doctors and ministers to check in on Ludwig.

The men argued over who should ride in which of the three carriages (well, actually two, since one was reserved for only Ludwig and a few attendants). Dr. Gudden insisted that the king's carriage must be made secure by removing the inside door latch so that Ludwig would not be able to escape. A commission member gave the castle saddler orders to prepare a carriage in this way. Becoming suspicious, the saddler spread news among other servants and townsfolk that something suspicious was going on.

The commissioners' dinner dragged on past midnight, and finally one member, Count Holnstein, was sent to the royal stables to secure transportation to Neuschwanstein. There, he ran into a coachman, who happened to be preparing Ludwig's horses for the king's night ride. When Holnstein announced to the coachman that a delegation from Munich had arrived to arrest the king, and that they needed transportation, the startled coachmen answered that he took orders from no one but the king.

"The king no longer commands! His Royal Highness Prince Luitpold is master!" Holnstein cried, exasperated. The entire delegation was feeling quite important, and didn't appreciate the little people thwarting their plans. The coachman fled the stables, hurrying up the steep mountain path to alert Ludwig at Neuschwanstein.

Instead of meeting the king with his horses and carriage, the coachman was alone and breathless when he arrived in Ludwig's rooms to share the bad news.

"It cannot be," muttered the disbelieving king. He believed his aides would have warned him of a coup attempt. Nonetheless, Ludwig ordered the castle gates closed and sent an attendant to the nearby village of Füssen to alert the police and fire brigade of possible trouble.

Around 3:00 a.m., the Munich commission made its way up the steep road to Neuschwanstein in their three carriages. Rain was pouring down, and when the men reached the castle, a brigade of soldiers who had just arrived from the village refused them entrance. Villagers had begun gathering at the castle as well, lining the path and shouting insults at the evil commissioners who had presumably come to take away their beloved king.

One woman was especially forceful in her behavior. Baroness von Truchsess was a prominent member of Munich society who shared a bond with the king in that Dr. von Gudden had declared each of them insane (presumably the doctor had actually examined the baroness, however). She had been fond of Ludwig for years, even going so far as to build a villa in the village of Hohenschwangau so she could be near him. Due to her social rank, von Truchsess knew each of the commission members. She now attacked them with her umbrella, shouting: "Your children will be ashamed of you! Are you not ashamed of betraying your king? A glorious legacy you will leave your children!"

Unlike the delegation members, the baroness was able to force her way into Neuschwanstein, where she eventually found Ludwig. She vowed to personally protect the king, crying out dramatically, "I shall not leave my king to these traitors!" She begged him to leave for Munich and appeal to his people for their support.

Ludwig was still in a state of denial over the coup. He was even a bit amused by the baroness's theatrical displays of devotion and alarm. But after an hour of listening to her, he grew tired and asked a servant to see her out. He was concerned over something she had told him: the names of the commission members. Ludwig was stunned to learn that some of them were ministers he had trusted. Furious, he demanded their arrest.

Outside in the downpour, the commission members attempted to protect themselves from the villagers, who had now turned out in full force to protect their beloved fairy king. Men, women, and children alike jeered at the delegation and threatened them with axes, pitchforks, swords, and rifles. The commissioners were shocked; the Munich crowds had never shown such affection for the king.

Police, with bayonets drawn, locked the commissioners into the castle gatehouse. One delegate escaped and fled to Munich to inform Prime Minister Lutz of events. The arrested men were alarmed when they heard Ludwig's plans for them. The king had flown into a rage, storming about Neuschwanstein's upper floors and ordering that the commissioners be chained, beaten, starved, skinned alive, have their eyes put out, and left to "decay in their own filth."

However, like most of Ludwig's other threats, this one proved short-lived. The men were released after just a few hours.

Meanwhile, in Munich, the regency of Prince Luitpold was declared that morning. The king became truly fearful for the first time when he heard this. Feeling the need for advice, he called in the aides and servants still remaining. Ludwig had ordered that his carriage and horse be prepared to take him to Munich. Bismarck had suggested this course of action as well, inferring that public goodwill would save Ludwig if he appeared before his people in the capital. But the king's aide, Dürckheim, feared that it was too late and that the king would be arrested when he entered Munich. He urged Ludwig to flee over the mountains into Austria instead, à la *The Sound of Music*. The border was not far away, and Austria's Emperor Franz Joseph was married to Ludwig's beloved cousin, Sisi.

Still, Ludwig's honor and respect for his royal office would not allow him to sneak away like a common prisoner. "My subjects shall judge whether I am crazy or not," he said, although he did attempt to reach out by composing telegrams to the Emperors of Germany and Austria, whom he thought might help him. But events were quickly spiraling out of the king's control. Munich authorities, instructed to now take orders from Prince Luitpold, intercepted and destroyed the telegrams.

Dürckheim encouraged Ludwig to write an appeal to the Bavarian people. The king did so, writing in part:

"I, Ludwig II, King of Bavaria, am under the necessity of addressing this appeal to my Faithful and beloved people, as well as to the whole German Nation. My Uncle, Prince Luitpold, designs, without My consent, to have himself proclaimed as Regent of My Kingdom, and My former Ministry has, by means of false reports about the state of My Health, deceived My Beloved People and thus rendered itself guilty of High Treason. I enjoy perfect health, and my Mind is as sound as that of any other Monarch, but the contemplated High Treason is so sudden and astounding that I have not had time to take the necessary measures to meet it, or to frustrate the criminal designs of My former Ministers.

"I enjoin every Bavarian Citizen, true to his King, to fight against Prince Luitpold and the Ministry until now in power, as against dangerous traitors. I have confidence in My People and feel sure they will not desert Me in the Hour of My Need."

Dürckheim had 10,000 copies of this address printed. He sought to deliver them to various newspapers and officials, but most were intercepted and never reached their intended audience. A Bamberg newspaper was one of the few places it appeared.

Above all, the rapidly-unfolding events were confusing and distressing to Ludwig. He was king! He was sovereign! God had appointed him to rule over the Bavarian people! Who could possibly have conspired to remove him from the throne? He dashed off his thoughts to his cousin, Prince Ludwig Ferdinand, whose baby he had recently visited. "I cannot think who is behind it," he wrote. "Someone must be. Can you discover? For some time I have known that people have been paid for going about saying that I am ill and unfit to rule. Such infamy."

The king should have followed his initial instinct and headed to Munich, but he felt paralyzed with indecision. Humiliated and depressed, he couldn't really believe that this whole nightmare was happening. He waited for fate to unfold, unable to act. During his deliberations, an armed contingent from the capital arrived at Neuschwanstein. At first, Ludwig was hopeful that they had come to protect him from his persecutors. He soon learned that their purpose was to prevent his escape. Ludwig was now a captive in a beautiful prison of his own creation.

Ludwig felt that even now, someone would surely come to his rescue. After all, he had seen hundreds of plays and operas where the brave, persecuted hero prevailed in the end. Right would surely triumph over might! "Here I am – a prisoner, without committing any crime!" he exclaimed to a servant. "What have I done to my subjects to be forsaken like this? Wretched king that I am, have I no friends to help me?"

The next morning, June 10, dawned brightly. The shining sun contrasted oddly with the chaos in the castle. Ludwig suffered yet another blow when his aide, Count Dürckheim, was summoned to Munich. Knowing how much the king relied on him, Dürckheim telegraphed Prince Luitpold, asking permission to remain with Ludwig. A swift reply threatened the count with charges of high treason should he stay with the king. Learning this, Ludwig insisted that Dürckheim return to the capital. "I realize you must go back, or your career and your future will be ruined," he said. As the aide left, Ludwig asked him to obtain poison for him from the nearest chemist. "You can get poison from anywhere. I cannot continue to live."

As evening fell, Ludwig's distress increased. His normal sleeping and waking times had been totally disrupted, and he had not slept for many hours. Only a few servants were left. They had heard the proclamation of Prince Luitpold as regent, and one by one had fled the castle to Munich. Ludwig was no longer the "winning team," and they feared for their future if they stayed on with him.

The Bavarian government had cut the phone lines and power supply to Neuschwanstein, but in a defiant show, Ludwig ordered the entire castle illuminated. Servants dashed down corridors, lighting torches and lanterns. The castle sent out an eerie glow across the valley below. Neuschwanstein stood as a lighthouse, perched high on its mountain foothills. But would it draw any hero to rescue the king? Would Lohengrin, the swan knight, arrive in time to save Ludwig as he had saved Elsa?

With growing speed and desperation, Ludwig paced the castle corridors. He drank increasingly throughout the evening, clenching and unclenching his fists and gesturing wildly as he contemplated his remaining hours of freedom. Desperation sank in as he realized that he was running out of time and ideas for a happy ending. His fairy castle, with its dark wood, rich colors, and striking gold, would do him no good if he were no longer king. He knew that he would never be able to return to his beloved castles again. To Ludwig, who had only lived as a member of royalty, life as an everyday person – and an insane one at that – was not worth living. From his balcony, he peered out across the mist-shrouded Alps he so loved. Scanning the gorgeous view, his eyes came to rest on Hohenschwangau, his childhood home where he had spent so many hours studying the beautiful murals and had fallen in love with his beloved German myths. He had hoped for a reign focused on beauty, but events had turned into something hideous and ugly. How had things gone so wrong? Ludwig turned his head toward the Pöllat Gorge with its waterfall pouring down the rocky cliff, and considered how he might end his life by jumping into it.

Ludwig summoned his valet, Mayr, and asked for the keys to the castle's highest tower. Mayr put off this request and told Ludwig that the keys were lost. Fearing a suicide attempt, and also considering his own future, Mayr made the decision to alert government officials in Munich. He sent a telegram informing them of the king's suicide threats.

Throughout the evening, Ludwig made increasingly hopeless remarks in the hearing of the servants: "Half-past twelve I was born and half-past twelve I shall die," "No blood shall be shed for my sake. I shall settle my account with Heaven," and finally, "I hope God will forgive me this step."

Just before midnight, the king called one of the remaining servants, Alfons Weber, to his study. He scrounged through drawers for all the money he could find, which he gave to Weber, as well as a diamond pin he liked to wear on his hats. "Here's my last, you deserve it, you've been the most loyal one. I shall need no more money," Ludwig told a tearful Weber. He also handed his well-used prayer book to the valet, saying, "Pray for me!"

Despite his talk of suicide, the king seemed to lack the will or energy to act on any plans. He was crushed not only by the apparent loss of his kingship, but even more by the report declaring him insane. "It is not the worst that they want to rob me of my throne," he told a servant. "But it will be the death of me that they want to have me declared insane and buried alive." Ludwig knew all too well the life that his brother Otto was living, and the thought of being confined like Otto terrified him. His mind frantically searched for some way of escape.

Time was running out for the king. Around midnight, the commission arrived at Neuschwanstein again. This time, there was no resistance, since all the guards and law enforcement knew by now that Ludwig was no longer in control.

Ludwig's servant Mayr had switched sides and was now working with the Bavarian government. He met the commissioners at the gate, and together the men devised a plan to trap Ludwig. Several members of the commission scurried away, posting themselves halfway up the tower steps. Mayr planned to tell the king that the tower keys had been found, and once Ludwig entered the tower, more commissioners would enter behind him, trapping him.

Mayr hurried off to tell the king that he had finally found the tower keys. Ludwig headed to the tower, turning the key in its cold latch one final time. Deliberately, he began to ascend the steps. But within seconds, he was startled to run into some of the commissioners.

More men came from both below and above, and two of them seized Ludwig roughly by the arms. Dr. Gudden stepped forward.

"Majesty, this is the saddest task that has ever fallen to my lot; Your Majesty's case has been studied by four specialists on madness, and from the report made by them Your Majesty's uncle, Prince Luitpold, has been entrusted with the Regency. I shall have the honor of conducting Your Majesty to the castle of Berg. We shall start this very night."

Stunned, Ludwig was silent for a moment. Then, he let out a long, agonizing groan before saying in a low voice, "What do you require me to do? What is the meaning of all this?"

The commissioners escorted the king back to his bedroom, and in an awful attempt at normalcy, Gudden introduced the members of the delegation. They included Count Holnstein, who had held a position of great importance in Ludwig's court in earlier years. By now, the king had had a few minutes to collect his thoughts.

"How can you certify me insane without seeing me and examining me beforehand?" he asked – an entirely reasonable question.

Gudden replied that "overwhelming" evidence of the king's mental illness was sufficient for him to make that judgment.

Frustrated and agitated, Ludwig paced back and forth, pondering how he could respond. He decided to appeal to Gudden's professional pride. "Listen, as an experienced neurologist, how can you be so devoid of scruple as to make out a certificate that is decisive for a human life? You have not seen me for the last twelve years!"

"I took this step on the strength of the servants' evidence," Gudden replied. Did he realize, even as the words escaped his lips, how weak this reasoning sounded as grounds for removing a king from his throne?

"Ah!" Ludwig cried. "On the strength of the evidence of these paid lackeys that I have raised from nothing and they betray me in return! Prince Luitpold has blissfully succeeded. He would not have needed such elaborate intelligence. Had he said just one word, I would have abdicated and gone abroad. And how long, assuming that I am really sick, do you think my cure will take?"

"That will depend upon Your Majesty," Gudden replied. "It will be necessary for Your Majesty to submit to my instructions."

At the word "submit," Ludwig was filled with rage. No one could tell the king to submit! "No Wittelsbach – let me tell you once and for all – need never submit to anything!" the king shouted.

Seeing that this conversation was leading nowhere, the commissioners moved out. Gudden instructed Ludwig to pack a few things for the journey to Berg Castle. As he was escorted to the second of three carriages making the journey, Ludwig whispered to a remaining staff member, "Preserve these rooms as a sacred precinct, and let no curious eyes profane them!" He asked Mayr for poison, and as he turned to gaze at his fairy tale castle one final time, he uttered, "Farewell Schwanstein, child of my sorrows!"

Then, wrapped in a dark coat and with a hat pushed low on his forehead, King Ludwig II climbed into his carriage. Several asylum wardens joined him there. As he rode down the steep descent from the castle, he peered out at a mass of villagers, raising their hats silently to him and tossing flowers at his carriage through the fog and rain. The crowd was subdued compared to the raucous group of a few days earlier. They knew that the die had been cast. This was farewell to their fairy tale king.

Police Sergeant Boppeler watched the procession leave from the gatehouse, recalling, "I shall never forget this funeral procession for a living ruler."

Inside his rolling prison, Ludwig was as deeply moved as he had been at any Wagner opera performance. He silently bowed to his subjects, showing his respect for how well they had played their roles.

CHAPTER 18

Ludwig and Dr. Gudden leave Berg Castle for a walk

THE CURTAIN FALLS

The carriages journeyed eight hours through the pouring rain, arriving at Berg around noon on June 12. Ludwig climbed out along the familiar path to the castle. He had stayed here so often over the years ... spent afternoons swimming in Starnberger See with Otto ... met Wagner, the Great Friend, here for the first time ... entertained Sophie here, so many years ago ... taken long walks with Sisi along this shore ... and now, his twenty-two-year reign was ending in humiliation here. Spotting a familiar face among the guards lining the path, Ludwig smiled. "Ah, Sauer, it's nice to see that you are in service here again." Perhaps, if the king just acted like normal, all this would turn out to be one long nightmare?

Inside the castle, Ludwig saw that the situation was all too real. The castle had been converted during the past few days into a prison impossible to escape. The regal furnishings were still there, but holes had been drilled into the window frames in preparation for iron bars to be added. Peepholes seemed to mock Ludwig from almost every door, depriving him of any private moments.

Everywhere he looked, Ludwig saw more insults to his royal dignity. He was suspicious of many of the unfamiliar castle personnel and feared an assassination attempt. This was his worst nightmare come true. He felt buried alive!

Having been awake for over twenty-four hours, an exhausted Ludwig finally went to sleep around 3:00 p.m. He asked a warden to wake him at midnight, but was dismayed when he was told that he now needed to keep "normal" hours. Ah, the irony that Ludwig must live "normally," in a castle prison!

Ludwig woke around 3:00 a.m. on June 13, ready to dress and prepare for his day. He requested clothes, only to be told he needed to go back to sleep. The restless king paced his room until boredom led him back to bed. Around 6:00 a.m., he rose again. This time, orderlies did bring clothes for him. But his request to attend mass at a nearby church was refused. This particularly bothered Ludwig, because it was Whitsunday, the day when the Holy Spirit empowered believers after Jesus' resurrection. The entire Whitsun weekend was a holiday in Germany, and to deny the king the right to attend church seemed cruel.

Ludwig asked for his personal hairdresser, who had arranged his hair each day of his reign. This was refused as well. Reluctantly, the king allowed an orderly to shave and dress him.

Outside Berg Castle, events in Bavaria were unfolding without the king's knowledge. His cousin Sisi, who was staying at her family home on Lake Starnberg, had been informed of Ludwig's arrest. This upset her greatly, and she kept a close eye on the news. In Munich, the mood was tense. Both police and the military were on high alert, fearing revolts and attempts to rescue the king. The commissioners were highly unpopular. The Austrian ambassador reported, "All lower classes are in support of the king. Merchants, contractors, servants and workers express violent views against the government, particularly against the commission. They don't believe in the king's illness."

Back at the castle, Ludwig spent the morning in conversations with Dr. Gudden and Gudden's son-in-law, Dr. Grashey. The king impressed both men with his calm demeanor. He asked many questions about his proposed course of treatment and possible cure, which involved living a life of moderation: keeping normal hours and cooperating with his doctors. No doubt Ludwig recognized this as the dreaded "moral treatment" that Otto had been subjected to for years. There would be no more private meals with Marie Antoinette or nighttime rides across his beloved countryside. He was to be treated as a child, and expected to live within the strict limits placed on him. But instead of raging against these affronts to his royal dignity, Ludwig seemed to accept most of Grashey's advice. Calmly, he asked that his books from Neuschwanstein be moved to Berg so that he could have reading material.

After their meeting, Grashey suggested to Dr. Gudden that Ludwig was not hopelessly incurable. Dr. Gudden quickly rebuffed him, commenting harshly that the king's illness, as a matter of record, was a permanent condition.

Around 11:30 that morning, Dr. Gudden suggested that Ludwig join him on an outdoor walk. The rain had finally lifted, and the doctor felt that nature would be good for the king. Ludwig joined him, and orderlies followed at a distance. Their presence alarmed Ludwig. He asked their identity, fearing that they might be assassins. Gudden assured the king that all was well.

Ludwig proceeded to exhaust the doctor with incessant questions as they walked among the trees. Upon returning to the castle, Gudden announced to the other doctors that Ludwig had impressed him with his calm demeanor. Gudden felt that his "treatment" was working quite well already, and remarked that the king seemed almost normal. Did he find it odd that less than twelve hours of his treatment could cause noticeable improvement in such a hopeless case? Did he have second thoughts concerning whether Ludwig was insane to begin with? We will never know. He sent a telegram to Prime Minister Lutz, informing him, "So far, everything here has gone marvelously."

During the afternoon, Ludwig was as focused as he had ever been in his life. Just what was he thinking? That's a mystery that we will never solve. Observers noted that he spent much time peering out the window. At times, he surveyed the lake with a telescope. Even the servants had noticed an unusually large number of boats sailing on Lake Starnberg that afternoon. What was Ludwig looking for? Regardless of any plans he may have been forming, it's certain that he viewed the area with sentimental memories. He gazed across the water to the Isle of Roses, where he had spent so many hours in blessed isolation. Now his eyes took in the many commoners, enjoying the freedom of a holiday weekend. Ah – freedom! Had he appreciated freedom while he had it? Would he ever be free again, in this life?

When an orderly checked in on him, Ludwig gave him a sealed note which he asked to be delivered to Sisi at Possenhofen, just across the lake. The king asked casually how many guards were on duty along castle grounds. Told that there were between six and eight, the king then asked whether they were armed. Ludwig seemed relieved to learn that they were not. The orderly noted that the king appeared a bit distressed. He attributed this to Ludwig's concern that the light rain could prevent his evening walk with Dr. Gudden.

At 4:30 p.m., Ludwig ate a huge meal, alone as usual. Accompanying it, he drank a glass of beer and seven glasses of wine. Was he steeling himself for events to come?

Dr. Gudden was not enthusiastic about taking an evening walk in the rain, and was further tired out by the king's constant questions whenever the two were together. However, he agreed to Ludwig's fervent wish to go walking. Wearing hats and coats over their suits, the two men departed the castle down the same path they had walked that morning. Both carried umbrellas. As they had done earlier, orderlies followed at a distance. But this time, inexplicably, Dr. Gudden waved off the orderlies almost immediately. Why? As an instructor, Dr. Gudden had cautioned his students to never go off alone with an insane patient. Yet this is exactly what he did with Ludwig.

Dr. Gudden planned to catch a train to Munich that night, and he told servants to expect the two back no later than 8:00 p.m. It was 6:25 as they disappeared from the castle's view.

Neither was ever seen alive again.

CHAPTER 19

Ludwig lies in state in the Residenz

"AN ETERNAL ENIGMA"

By 9:00 p.m., Dr. Müller was worried. Eight o'clock had come and gone, and still there was no sign of Ludwig or Dr. Gudden. At first, Dr. Müller thought that the men might be taking shelter from the rain, which had grown heavier. But it was not at all like the punctual Dr. Gudden to be an hour late. Müller arranged a search party to scan the park surrounding the castle. Armed with torches and lanterns, the men ventured out into the dark, wet night. Although it was difficult to see much in the windy, rainy gloom, the searchers made a thorough canvas of the grounds and found nothing.

Dr. Müller began to panic. If the men weren't in the park, what had happened? Had Ludwig tried to escape? Surely Dr. Gudden wouldn't have allowed that … could they possibly be in the lake? Müller shuddered to consider the possibilities. Reluctantly, he expanded the search to Lake Starnberg. Around 10:00 p.m., a footman's shout rang out into the night. He had found Ludwig's hat by the water's edge! Other search party members hurried over to the spot, about a half-mile from the castle at a place where the path veered near the lake. In short order they discovered Gudden's coat and his hat, which was crushed. Nearby lay the king's coat and suit jacket. These must have been removed quickly, as the sleeves were turned inside out and the suit jacket was still inside the overcoat. All the clothing was lying on shore, drenched. Ludwig's umbrella turned up near a bench a short distance away.

With trepidation, but with adrenaline flowing, Dr. Müller and the assistant castle steward hopped into a small boat and pushed off from shore. Within minutes, the steward cried out. He saw a dark object floating among the reeds about ten feet from shore!

The men pulled a stroke ahead.

It was clear that the object was a body.

They pulled a stroke closer.

The body was facedown, with arms outstretched.

Another stroke.

The hair was dark. Trembling, they turned the body over. It was Ludwig, eyes staring vacantly ahead. His feet anchored in the mud and stones at the lake's bottom, he floated gently in water just four feet deep. Nearby, they discovered the body of Dr. Gudden, in a half-sitting position with his back underwater. His feet were entangled in mud and stones on the bottom of the lake, just as the king's had been. His watch, now stopped, read 8:00.

In shocked silence, the searchers pulled the bodies into the boat and rowed them back to shore, where they laid them. A crowd of servants had gathered, and the head cook and butler insisted that both the king and Dr.

Gudden showed faint signs of life! Energized, Dr. Müller and some attending policemen worked feverishly to perform mouth-to-mouth resuscitation on both Ludwig and Dr. Gudden. But after nearly an hour of this, the men gave up, seeing no results. Just after midnight, Müller pronounced Ludwig II, King of Bavaria, dead at age forty.

Servants wrapped both bodies in blankets and carried them inside for a final time, retracing the path the men had walked just hours before.

It was noted that Dr. Gudden's face was marred with a number of scratches, a large bruise over his right eye, and a deep gash in his forehead. The nail of one finger on his right hand had been nearly torn off. Regardless of the form death had taken, Gudden had apparently fought hard against it.

Ludwig's body showed no signs of struggle, eerily confirming his words to a servant just days before at Neuschwanstein: "Drowning is a fine death. There is no mutilation of the body." His pocket watch, dangling from his waistcoat pocket, had water between the face and glass. It had stopped at 6:54.

The next morning, Monday, June 14, the two bodies were laid out at Berg Castle, in separate rooms. Experts visited the king's body to make a death mask, a plaster cast of his face. This was a common practice at the time, used to preserve leaders' features for the future, since photography was just coming into widespread use. They also made casts of Ludwig's hands.

Police guards were on duty to keep out a swarm of tourists, eager to see their king one final time. Ludwig's closest friend, Sisi, knew of his incarceration at Berg, and was utterly despondent upon hearing that he had died. "The king was no madman, only an eccentric living in a world of dreams!" she cried to her mother, who was staying with her at their summer home on Lake Starnberg. "They might have treated him more gently and spared him such a terrible end." The death of the king, whose personality had been so similar to hers, shook her to the core. "He is not really dead!" she exclaimed upon seeing the corpse, sobbing uncontrollably. "My dear, dear

Ludwig! It is only pretense: all he wants is to be left in peace – not to be persecuted any longer!" She requested that her ladies-in-waiting leave her alone with Ludwig once more. She placed a red rose on his pillow, and when her attendants later peeked in, they found the Empress unconscious on the floor next to the bed.

The public shared Sisi's grief. Ludwig's deposition and death had come so suddenly and so unexpectedly that most Bavarians were caught totally off guard. It was similar, in some ways, to the sudden and shocking death of Britain's Princess Diana 100 years later, in 1997.

A carriage conducted Ludwig's body back to Munich, the city he had done so much to avoid during life. Bavarians living near Lake Starnberg had nearly covered the carriage in flowers and wreaths. On its trip, the coach passed by Fürstenried, where Ludwig's brother Otto was technically now King of Bavaria. When a delegation informed Otto of his brother's death, the new king accepted the news without emotion and changed the subject. As the carriage neared Munich's center, more and more Bavarians joined the procession, walking silently behind their fallen leader.

Ludwig's body was dressed in the regal uniform of the Knights of Saint Hubertus and laid into a casket for viewing in the resplendent Old Chapel of the Residenz. His left hand clutched the hilt of a sword; his right, a small bouquet of white jasmine gathered by Sisi. She knew that jasmine was one of his favorite flowers. His casket lay on a bier covered with royal ermine robes that he would never again wear. The chapel walls were draped in black, and a canopy of black silk attached to the ceiling center fell in billows to each of the four corners of the room. Above the altar hung a white cross and the Wittelsbach coat of arms.

In death, as in life, Ludwig was surrounded with the candles, flowers, and the floral scents that he loved. Potted laurel and cypress trees filled the room, along with thousands of flowers of every kind. Hundreds of tall votive candles surrounded the casket, casting a haunting glow against the black walls. The flames flickered and danced as thousands of mourners passed by to pay their respects and to see their king up close. Days earlier, this prospect would have unnerved Ludwig, but he was now blissfully unaware of the curious eyes gazing at his every detail: the ruffles at his neck or the upswept hair, curled for a final time.

A newspaper reported, "The crush of mourning folk to the Old Chapel in the Residenz was without end. A lady who had fainted was almost trampled to death. Yesterday a total of twenty people fainted and a mountain of lost tresses, bustles, and broken umbrellas bore testimony to the rigors to which people subjected themselves."

Even outside the chapel, it was impossible to miss the signs that Munich was a city in mourning. Buildings were draped in black crepe, flags flew at half-mast, and church bells tolled as a reminder to residents to pray for the departed king's soul. The thunder of cannons ripped through the air in a final tribute to Ludwig.

Saturday, June 19, dawned sunny and warm. The heavens seemed to signal that the great tragedy of the past week had passed, and that Ludwig was to find the rest and solitude he craved at last. His funeral was the largest state occasion ever held in Munich, with thousands lining the route to see eight white horses pull the hearse through the streets. His favorite horse followed, its empty saddle draped in black. Prince Luitpold walked solemnly behind the carriage as well.

The journey from the Residenz to Saint Michael's church, a distance of less than a mile and a half, was expanded to a winding route lasting two and a half hours in order to accommodate all the mourners wishing to say goodbye. After a brief service in the soaring Renaissance church, monks carried the casket down a flight of stone steps into the crypt, where Ludwig joined a row of several other Wittelsbach relatives. You can see his casket there still today.

As the monks descended the stairs, the sky suddenly grew overcast, and a giant bolt of lightning split the sky, nearly striking the church. "The heavens shed a tear," a newspaper suggested.

Ludwig's body was missing one component: his heart. In accordance with tradition, the heart was removed and sent to Altötting, a village known as "the heart of Bavaria." Its Chapel of the Miraculous Image contains twenty-eight silver vases, each holding the heart of a Wittelsbach ruler. There, Ludwig's restless heart found its place of final repose, along with those of his father, grandfather, and other ancestors.

CHAPTER 20

Cross on Lake Starnberg marks the spot where Ludwig was found

WHAT REALLY HAPPENED?

What really happened on the night of June 13? The events have remained shrouded in mystery ever since; after all, the only two eyewitnesses – Ludwig and Dr. Gudden – were dead. Security cameras had not been invented, and anyone else who may have witnessed the deaths wasn't talking.

The Bavarian government, with Prime Minster Lutz in power and Prince Luitpold serving as a figurehead king, was anxious to put any suspicion to rest. They glossed over early reports that Ludwig and Dr. Gudden had shown possible signs of life when discovered, and reported that both were already dead when they were found. The official report also speculated that the most likely scenario involved Ludwig hitting Dr. Gudden in the head with his umbrella (thereby causing the gash on his forehead), drowning him while he was unconscious, and then drowning himself.

Eager to report any findings that would confirm their diagnosis of Ludwig's insanity, they also noted that an autopsy found the king's brain chronically inflamed and weighing 1349 grams. This was thirty-six grams less than average, and both the inflammation and the size were inferred as signs of mental weakness. However, many details of the autopsy were never made public, and several sources denied that an autopsy even took place.

Among the general public, rumors ran rampant. Many felt Ludwig had tried to escape. Ludwig's cousin Karl Theodor, Sisi's brother, held this opinion. A number of signs pointed toward this conclusion. After the night's events, it was discovered that many of the boats seen on Lake Starnberg that day held armed men from nearby towns who were ready to help the king escape. Sisi spent the afternoon of June 13 wandering the shore at Possenhofen, just across the lake from Berg. She insisted on remaining outside even into the rainy evening. Did the note Ludwig had delivered to her that afternoon spell out his plans for an escape attempt? More rumors speculated that Sisi had a carriage waiting to whisk Ludwig away. Indeed, unexplained carriage tracks were found in the mud near shore the next day. A nearby stable held ten horses rather than the usual two. And Richard Hornig, a former valet of the king's, was later reported to have stood near the lake by the castle, ready with a boat. If Ludwig did first remove Dr. Gudden as an impediment by knocking him unconscious with the umbrella, he probably then tried to swim to a rescue boat, a waiting carriage, or Possenhofen. Sisi's summer home on the lake was a swim of just over a mile. Ludwig was a strong swimmer and had swum this distance many times. However, he had just eaten a large meal, and the lake waters were cold. The peace-loving monarch was also under stress from his fight with Dr. Gudden and from anxiety over the many pieces that would need to come together in order to complete this rescue. Perhaps it was all too much, and he suffered a heart attack and drowned. It's extremely unlikely that he drowned accidentally, as the water where he was found was only four feet deep.

The escape theory seems more likely than a suicide theory, since Ludwig had had many opportunities for suicide at Neuschwanstein, and yet had not acted on them. Why would he have finally killed himself on the evening of June 13, and not before?

Another theory holds that Ludwig began his escape attempt, and then Dr. Gudden pulled out a bottle of chloroform he had been carrying. Chloroform was a crude anesthetic used at that time, and proponents of this idea suggest that the doctor accidentally killed Ludwig with an overdose of the drug, and then suffered a heart attack himself from the shock. However, no chloroform bottle or handkerchief from which to inhale it were found at the scene.

The men's watches were another source of confusion. Ludwig's stopped at 6:54, Gudden's at 8:00. What scenario could place Ludwig's death more than an hour before Gudden's? Some have speculated that Gudden simply forgot to wind his watch earlier in the day, and that it had been stopped since 8:00 that morning. However, others counter that Gudden was a meticulous man and therefore don't find this theory believable. Like much other evidence from that night, the watches have disappeared from history.

Some Bavarians saw more sinister forces at work, and they suspected that the men had been assassinated. Jacob Lidl, one of the searchers on June 13, left a deathbed statement of "something mysterious" that had happened that night. Friends later confided that Lidl had seen Ludwig shot while trying to escape into a boat. This statement mysteriously disappeared, but Lidl's relatives have kept the tale alive by passing it down through the generations via word of mouth. It's not inconceivable that Ludwig was assassinated. Cabinet members were no doubt relieved when the beloved Fairy Tale King was permanently silenced and out of the picture after their coup removing him from power. There was no official investigation after Ludwig's death, and the government hushed any news deviating from the official line. Of course, this just led to further rumors and speculation.

Was Ludwig killed? Rudolf Magg, a doctor called to Berg after the two bodies were discovered, made a stunning deathbed confession to his daughter. According to Magg, high-level officials had forced him to give false testimony that Ludwig had drowned. In reality, Magg said that the king's body had conclusive bullet wounds.

Then there is Princess Theresa, the daughter of Prince Luitpold, who now ruled in Ludwig's place. Theresa had always had a soft spot for her cousins Ludwig and Otto. She had been fond of Otto for years, and some say the reason she never married was because Otto was her first and only true love. Even after Otto was confined to Fürstenried, Theresa continued to write to him and deplored the way the family had treated him. She went on to become a serious botanist. Regarding Ludwig, she wrote, "The overwhelming feeling I had that Ludwig II did not want to end his life but had intended to flee, was later confirmed to me by a most trustworthy individual. It is important that I record the facts in writing for all times.

"A powerful lady who happened to be staying at Lake Starnberg at the time, had secretly put the escape plan into action and notified the king about this. On the evening of June 13 a small boat was waiting not far from the garden fence at Castle Berg, to rescue the fleeing man." The "powerful lady" mentioned was no doubt Sisi.

In 2007, more shadows from the past emerged when Detlev Utermöhle, a retired Munich banker, went public with a tale from his youth. As a ten-year-old, he and his mother had visited Countess Josephine von Wrba-Kaunitz, who was caretaker to some of the Wittelsbach family's assets. She whispered to Utermöhle and his mother, "Now you will find out the truth about Ludwig's death without his family knowing. I will show you all the coat he wore on the day he died."

She pulled a gray overcoat from a chest, and showed them two bullet holes in its back. The banker's mother wrote about this incident as well. But the coat is no longer around. It burned in a 1973 house fire which also killed the Countess and her husband.

So while much hearsay tends to support the idea that Ludwig was killed, there is no hard evidence. Lidl's notebook, Ludwig's overcoat, the note Ludwig sent to Sisi the afternoon of his death – all have vanished into the murky past. Some have suggested that Ludwig's body be exhumed and examined, but the Wittelsbach family has strongly opposed this. They have always denied any assassination rumors. Perhaps this isn't surprising, since the surviving Wittelsbachs are not direct descendants of either Ludwig or Otto – they are from the lines of Prince Luitpold and Ludwig's other aunts and uncles. Like the Kennedy assassination, Ludwig's death seems destined to be forever shrouded in mystery.

Ludwig probably wouldn't mind. "I feel so forsaken and lonely on this earth, like a leftover from better times, blown into the present which I hate, and where I shall always feel a stranger," he once wrote. "I wish to remain an eternal enigma, to myself and to others."

Soldiers remove looted artwork from Neuschwanstein after WWII

EPILOGUE

The day after Ludwig's death, supporters anchored a pole in Lake Starnberg at the spot where his body was found. Today, a memorial stone chapel looks down onto the still water from a nearby hillside. It's all so calm and peaceful that it's hard to believe the Fairy Tale King died here. Admirers still gather each June on the anniversary of Ludwig's death, proudly wearing their bright Bavarian dirndls and lederhosen. Silently, they cast wreaths, Bavarian flags, and Wittelsbach banners onto the water to remember the unforgettable life and mysterious death of King Ludwig.

Ludwig's mother, Queen Marie, was distraught upon learning of her son's unexpected death. She was now basically alone, since she could not bear to visit her remaining son, Otto, in his condition. She died three years after Ludwig.

Otto lived thirty more years, in splendid imprisonment at Fürstenried. A newspaper report told of his penchant for smoking (up to thirty-six cigarettes each day), and of his daily routine, arranged in the "painful detail" that Ludwig had mercifully avoided. Ironically, Otto became the longest-reigning Wittelsbach ruler ever. Although he likely never realized it, he held the title King of Bavaria for thirty years. He died in 1916 of a stomach hemorrhage.

Prince Luitpold, Ludwig's uncle who took over after Ludwig had been dethroned, lived on the third floor of Hohenschwangau castle after Queen Marie died. He reigned until his death in 1912, and the next year Hohenschwangau was opened as a museum. Luitpold's son then reigned as King Ludwig III until 1918, when World War I ended with Germany defeated and disgraced. German Kaiser Wilhelm II abdicated his throne, and the Wittelsbach rule of Bavaria came to an end as well.

What about Sophie, Ludwig's one-time fiancée? She married the French Duke of Alençon and had two children. In 1897, when Sophie was fifty, she was working at a charity bazaar in Paris when a fire broke out. Sophie died in the fire, trying to rescue all the girls who were working with her.

Sophie's sister Sisi, Ludwig's soul mate, had her own "not so happily ever after" ending. Sisi had difficult relationships with each of her four children, once saying, "Children are the curse of a woman, for when they come, they drive away beauty, which is the best gift of the gods." One daughter died as a toddler, and two others failed to interest her (similar in many ways to Ludwig's parents' lack of interest in their own children). Sisi smothered the final child, Valerie, with too much affection. Less than three years after Ludwig's death, Sisi's married son, Austrian Crown Prince Rudolf, shot and killed both himself and his mistress. This was a tragedy for more than just Sisi's family. Since Rudolf was Franz Joseph and Sisi's only son, succession then passed to Franz Joseph's brother and then his son, Archduke Ferdinand. This led to a series of events destabilizing the country, eventually resulting in the assassination of Archduke Ferdinand in 1914 and the beginning of World War I.

As for Sisi herself, she and husband Franz Joseph had never been especially close, but they became even more distant after Rudolf's death. Sisi was murdered in Geneva, Switzerland, in a bizarre incident in 1898. Sixty-year-old Sisi and a lady-in-waiting were walking from their hotel to catch a ferry at the dock. Suddenly, a young man ran up to the women. He seemed to stumble and threw out his arms as if to regain his balance. But although Sisi didn't immediately realize it, the man had stabbed her with a four-inch long file that he had inserted into a wooden handle. The man, an Italian anarchist, had planned to assassinate a ruler, but having missed that opportunity, decided to target Sisi. He had read in a newspaper that she was in town.

Unsure of what had happened, Sisi collapsed but was helped back to her feet by a bystander. She and her lady-in-waiting continued walking to the ferry, which they boarded. Sisi lost consciousness, and a doctor on board examined her and noted a small bloodstain on her chest. By the time she could be brought back to her hotel, thirty-five minutes after the attack, she was dead. An autopsy discovered that the file had penetrated Sisi's rib, lung, and heart. Because the file was so thin, and because of Sisi's typically tight corset, the blood leaking into the sac around her heart was slowed greatly, accounting for the amount of time she was able to live after the attack. Sisi had been Empress of Austria, reluctantly, for forty-four years.

What became of the buildings in our tale? Possenhofen, Sisi and Sophie's home on Lake Starnburg, became a children's home in the 1920s. Today, it has been converted into luxury apartments. You can still visit its grounds.

The Nazis occupied Berg Castle during World War II, ousting Wittelsbach family members, who opposed the Nazi party. Nazis stole most of the castle's priceless artwork and gutted much of the building, making it over as a school to educate girls in Nazi principles. Members of the Wittelsbach family ended up in concentration camps for part of the war, but survived. After the war, they reclaimed Berg, and it is still used as one of their homes. Ludwig III's grandson died there in 1996.

The Royal Family's official Munich home, the Residenz, was badly damaged during bombing in World War II. Most of it has been restored and you can visit it today, although Ludwig's grand Winter Garden was demolished in 1897.

Despite Ludwig's wishes to protect his castle from "curious eyes," Neuschwanstein, Linderhof, and Herrenchiemsee were all opened to the public on August 1, 1886 – just seven weeks after his death. By 1899, proceeds from visitors to the castles had paid off all the outstanding debt. Today, millions tour Ludwig's monuments to beauty each year, and the castles have brought far more money to Bavaria than the king ever spent building them. The "Mad King" is no longer a burden to the treasury. The Nazis used Neuschwanstein during World War II as a place to store artwork they looted from France.

When you visit Neuschwanstein, you will reach the different rooms by climbing steps in the main tower, whose keys were once "lost." As you wind your way up the stairs, linger for a moment. Can you sense a bit of Ludwig's presence, here in the place where commission members arrested him so many years ago?

Sisi continued to feel her cousin's spirit after his death. Is it possible she experienced him even more vividly? She told her niece this tale, which she called "true, every word of it":

The moon had risen and the moonlight made the room as bright as day. I watched as the door slowly opened and Ludwig came in.

His clothes were heavy with water, which dripped off him and formed little pools on the parquet floor. His wet hair was plastered round his white face, but it was clearly Ludwig, just as he had looked when he was alive.

We stared at one another in silence and then the king said, slowly and sadly, 'Are you afraid of me, Sisi?'

'No, Ludwig, I'm not afraid.'

'Oh dear,' he sighed, 'death has brought me no rest, Sisi. She is burning to death in agony. The flames flicker round her, she chokes on the smoke, she is burning to death and I cannot save her.'

'Who is burning to death, dear cousin?' I asked.

'I do not know, for her face is hidden,' he replied, 'but I do know that it is a woman who has loved me and until her fate is decided, I will not be free. But afterwards, you will encounter us and we three will be happy together in paradise.'

'How am I to know that I am not dreaming?' I asked.

Ludwig slowly approached my bed, the coldness of death and of the grave gave a chill to the air. 'Give me your hand,' he commanded.

I stretched out my hand and his wet fingers enclosed them. At that moment, I cried, 'Do not leave your friend, who loves you, to return to your suffering. Oh Ludwig, pray with me that you shall have your peace.'

But while I was speaking, the figure disappeared.

Bibliography

This book has been written based on the author's wide reading about the king, from sources including the following:

Baumer, Dorothea. *Guide to the Castles.* Garmisch-Patenkirchen: Fotoverlad Huber.

Bertram, Werner. *A Royal Recluse, Ludwig II.* Munich: Herpich, 1936.

Blunt, Wilfrid. *The Dream King.* New York: The Viking Press, 1970.

Chapman-Huston, Desmond. *Ludwig II, The Mad King of Bavaria.* New York: Dorset Press, 1990.

Desing, Julius. *King Ludwig II, His Life, His End.* Lechbruck: Verlag Kienberger, 1976.

Desing, Julius. *Royal Castle Neuschwanstein.* Wilhelm Kienberger GmbH, 1992.

Gerard, Frances. *The Romance of Ludwig II of Bavaria.* New York: Dodd, Mead & Co., 1901.

King, Greg. *The Mad King, A Biography of Ludwig II of Bavaria.* Secaucus, New Jersey: Birch Lane Press, 1996.

McIntosh, Christopher. *Ludwig II of Bavaria, The Swan King*. London: I. B. Tauris Publishers, 1982.

Merkle, Ludwig. *Sissi, The Tragic Empress*. Munich: Bruckmann, 1998.

Also by Susan Barnett Braun

I Love to Tell the Story: Growing Up Blessed and Baptist in Small Town Indiana

Kate Middleton, Duchess of Cambridge: A Biography for Young Readers

Kindle Books for Young Readers:

Sophie, Pay Attention (Rhoda, You Too)!

A Dog Called Naaman